KNACK
MAKE IT EASY

# INDIAN
# COOKING

KNACK

# INDIAN
# COOKING

## A Step-by-Step Guide to Authentic Dishes Made Easy

## MEENAKSHI AGARWAL

## Photography by Peter Ardito and Susan Byrnes

Guilford, Connecticut
An imprint of Globe Pequot Press

Copyright © 2010 by Morris Book Publishing, LLC

Editor in Chief: Maureen Graney
Editor: Katie Benoit
Cover Design: Paul Beatrice, Bret Kerr
Interior Design: Paul Beatrice
Layout: Casey Shain
Cover Photos by Peter Ardito and Susan Byrnes
All Interior Photos by Peter Ardito and Susan Byrnes with the exception of p. 25 (right) © Bygestudio/Dreamstime.com

Library of Congress Cataloging-in-Publication Data is available on file.

ISBN 978-1-59921-618-8

Printed in China

10 9 8 7 6 5 4 3 2 1

## Dedication

To my parents, for molding me into who I am today. To my husband, Atul, for adding flavor to my life.

## Acknowledgments

Maureen and Katie, you are rock stars, and I couldn't have brought life to this project without you. My friends and family, you are always ready to taste anything out of my kitchen with a smile on your face! And most importantly, to my blog readers, who inspire me to always keep cooking. I thank you all for your love and support. Happy eating!

Meena Agarwal
(www.hookedonheat.com)

## Photographers' Acknowledgments

The pungent fragrances of the Indian kitchen are still fresh in our memories as we write these words. Many thanks to all for making this project a success: Maureen Graney for selecting us to be part of this wonderful project. To Meena Agarwal for creating tasty dishes that delight both the palate and the eye. To our food stylist Grace Kwon for her skill and patience. Her contributions were invaluable.

Peter Ardito and Susan Byrnes,
Ardito + Byrnes Photography

# CONTENTS

# INTRODUCTION

One of the earliest and fondest memories I have of my childhood involves playing house with my younger brother and sister. We would think up make-believe scenarios and play them out to the best of our ability and conviction. Some of my favorite playtimes included those where I imagined myself in front of a running camera while I animatedly went through my very own cooking show. Yes, I could say that I was born with a spatula in place of one of my bones.

## Growing Up in the Middle East

I grew up with my two siblings, a younger brother and sister, in Kuwait, where my parents had made themselves feel at home for the past thirty years. Like every young liberal minded adult of their time, with dreams to see the other side of the world they grew up in, they both traveled the distance to this small desert country to find new purpose to their lives, and in turn, a better and brighter future than what they had succumbed to in their homelands. Amidst new opportunities and adventures, they found each other, and thus began the fusion of two cultures.

My mom is a Malaysian; my dad, an Indian. Theirs is, of course, a union of two very distinct cultures. Because my dad refused to forsake his *dal-roti* routine when he married my mom, she could never accept that cooking a traditional Indian meal was out of her reach. So she toiled, and she toiled, and today she makes better curries and meaner biryanis than any born-Indian I know.

Growing up, I truly believed that my mom was the best cook in the world. Many years later, I still hold strong to that belief. I loved watching her go about her kitchen duties while she chopped and prepped for dinner.

The year I turned fifteen, Mom thought it was about time I learned to cook. If nothing else, it would at least ensure that I could feed myself when the need arose. She started off with teaching me to boil an egg. Somehow, boiling the perfect egg was always a daunting task. Many weeks, and dozens of parboiled eggs later, she decided she had had enough. A girl doesn't need to live on boiled eggs—there is a whole world out there for her to explore that has nothing in particular to do with boiled eggs. Nonetheless, she decided to stick with eggs, only this time, fried. And glory to all glories, I nailed it from the get-go. With fried eggs being my favorite on the breakfast menu, Mom could now sleep peacefully knowing that when morning came, I could happily feed myself.

## To India for College

After high school, it was time for me to move into a hostel for my college years in India. This was to begin a whole new phase in my life. India seemed more alien to me than I had ever imagined, far from the comfort and security of the only home I had known until this time, Kuwait. Even though we spent almost every summer in Delhi and its surrounding areas, I still felt like a stranger in this new land. I had never before been to Bangalore, a modern, open-minded metropolitan city in the state of Karnataka towards the southern part of the Indian subcontinent. Here, I met many challenges, language being one of them. Food came a close second.

India is as diverse in its food as it is in its people. If you were to start from the very top, which is the state of Kashmir, and move slowly downward, stopping in every state, province, and major city, you would be surprised by the variety of food you would have tasted along the way. A simple meal of lentils, which is one of the staples in an Indian diet, has as many variations to it as the number of homes that cook them. While I loved my north Indian fare, the food of the south was totally new to me, and striking to my palate.

When I moved into college housing, I had very little in my recipe repertoire to equip me for an easy student life,

as far as food was concerned. I had to myself a tiny studio apartment, equipped with a working kitchen, but like any carefree college student, I foolishly thought I could survive on cheap takeout and meals served at the cafeteria. Many tasteless meals and an empty wallet later, I decided to take matters into my own hands. I called up my mom (the long-distance phone call that would soon become a weekly ritual, much to the chagrin of my dad over the never-ending phone bills) and told her of my plight. She asked me to grab a pen and some paper and take notes as she spoke. She gave me a list of things I needed to buy, and told me what to do with each of them.

I was to follow Mom's instructions to the letter at first, and once I felt the slightest bit of confidence, I could try to experiment on my own. But I was to always, and she meant *always*, call her back after each experiment and let me know what became of it. We would then discuss the process and find ways of perfecting it.

## Food and Family

Since the day I made that fateful call to my mom, and went and got groceries by myself for the first time ever, I never looked back. We still have our weekly long-distance calls—I now well settled into my own home in Canada and her happy in the comforts of her home in Kuwait—and discuss the food we cooked and ate. I continue to ask her for her opinions on the foods I intend to cook and for feedback on those that I put up on my blog.

When I look back, I always seem to remember food as something that brought our family together. Whenever we were happy or had any big news to share, food would most definitely become the center of our attention. I remember most of our birthday celebrations not by the gifts we received, but by the feast my mom made for us. Trips home from college during the summer were often preceded by many telephone calls planning the menu for the day I arrived. Most of our weekends were spent entertaining friends and family.

On a whim one rainy day, my food blog, Hooked on Heat (www.hookedonheat.com), was born. The domain name was gifted to me by my husband after we realized that a couple of months of blogging had gained me quite the fanfare. When I typed my first few words that fateful day, little did I know what impact it would have on my life. What began as an outlet for my passion turned into a career I had always dreamt of having.

## The Simple Basics

Of the few complaints I get about Indian cooking, the one that stands out is the myth that it is just too hard. Now, before you roll your eyes at me and say, "Yeah, sure, easy for you—you're Indian!" just hear me out. True, I was born Indian in an Indian household with a mom who cooks the most delicious Indian food I know, but truth be told, and as much as I would like to believe otherwise, I wasn't born with Indian culinary instincts in me. Yes, like any of you not familiar with South Asian cuisine, I too started off without much knowledge.

Try as I might, it's quite hard to convince people of just how simple and quick—and not to mention, healthy—Indian food can be. And this is where I intend this book to help out and introduce you to the simple basics of cooking Indian.

Most of us lead very busy lives these days, running from one commitment to another. If it's not work, then it's our family or friends who demand our time. While we all try to eat as best and as healthy as we can, more often than not we seem to find ourselves in a rut during meal times. As much as we'd like to, not many of us are willing to put in the time and effort that our moms seemed to easily put into their daily cooking.

My recipes are inspired by classic flavors and dressed up to suit our modern tastes. When it comes to fusion cooking, I am always one to experiment with the East and West. Somehow the exotic flavors of the East combined with the elegance of the West bring about the best of both worlds. While I'd like to believe that my book will be the first of its kind, the truth may be far from it. What I can promise you, however, is that it will be the best of its kind.

# POTS & PANS

## Picking the right pots and pans will make the cooking process more simple and fun

Indian cooking does not really require any special equipment. For the most part, you can more often than not make do with the standard pots and pans that you probably already have in your kitchen.

In most cases, standard nonstick cookware will work wonderfully with most of the recipes. Some recipes, however,

like those that require deep-frying, would fare much better in pots made of aluminum, like those traditionally used in India.

Always invest in good-quality cookware that will last you a lifetime, and make note to follow the usage and cleaning instructions properly to keep them in good shape. Avoid

### Deep Nonstick Pan with Lid

- If possible, get one in two different sizes, preferably small (1 liter) and medium (3 quarts). However, if you can only pick one, go for the medium size.

- Try to choose a pan with a glass lid so that you can peek into it without lifting

- the lid and letting the heat out while the food cooks.

- Use this pan for cooking curries, lentils, or vegetables that require a bit of simmer time.

- The nonstick coating makes this a great choice for cooking rice dishes like pilaf.

### Deep Heavy-Bottomed Pot

- Choose a pot that is at least 6 to 8 quarts in capacity.

- This kind of pot is perfect for slow-cooking meat curries as well as rich soups and stews that require a bit sautéing followed by simmering.

- A good choice for a heavy-bottomed pot like this is a Dutch oven that can go from the stove top to a preheated oven.

metal utensils that will scratch the pan.

For a beginner, it's very easy to go overboard and buy a whole set of pieces that you may not even need. Always look for pieces that can do double duty to save money and storage space. Also keep in mind the quantity of food you usually cook while picking out pots and pans. A 10-quart deep pan may be appealing if you're cooking for a large crowd, but if you only entertain and cook for four people at a time, it may not be such a good idea.

## Nonstick Wok with Lid

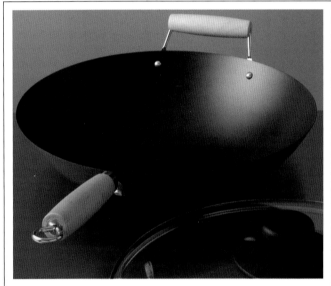

- Traditional Indian woks are usually made of thick aluminum and are known as *kadhais*.

- Using a nonstick wok will enable you to cut down on the amount of oil used while cooking.

- If given a choice, pick one with a glass lid and a single long handle, as opposed to one with handles on both sides, to make it easier to grip the wok while cooking.

- Use the wok especially for dishes that require a quick sauté or stir-fry.

## Nonstick Frying Pan

- A good-quality nonstick frying pan can easily substitute for the more traditional *tawa*.

- A nonstick frying pan is the perfect choice for shallow frying, but it is also a great option for making roti or any griddled Indian bread.

- A medium-size one would work well in most kitchens. However, you may want to invest in a larger size depending on the number of people you usually cook for.

# UTENSILS
## Pick utensils that work best for you and fit with your style of cooking

Using the right utensils can make a huge difference in the cooking process. Always pick ones that are comfortable and easy for you to use. Choose utensils based on the size of your pots and pans, and make sure they are long enough to keep your hands away from the rim of the pots to prevent any accidents.

These days there are so many different types of cooking utensils to choose from, in a wide range of sizes, shapes, and materials. Most of them are multipurpose and can be used in a variety of ways. By selecting utensils that are compatible with most of the cookware you own, it will be much easier to invest in higher quality products.

When picking utensils, always keep in mind the kind of cookware you intend to use them with, and opt for ones with

### Sharp Knives

- It is best to choose knives that you really need rather than invest in a set that contains some knives that you may never use.
- Make sure that your knives are sharpened regularly to make chopping and slicing as easy a process as possible.

### Cooking Tongs

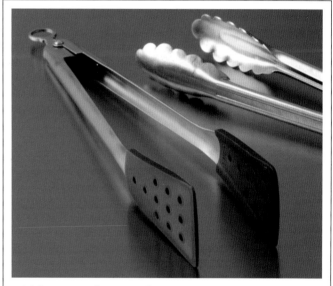

- It's best to opt for a pair of tongs large enough to use for sautéing as well as with the oven.
- Be sure to select a material that works well with nonstick pans and resists high heat.

a high heat resistance. It's very frustrating to see the tip of your spatula start to melt in contact with the hot pan, not to mention quite dangerous. Investing in high-quality utensils, although a little more expensive, will ensure that they last and perform well.

As with pots and pans, Indian cooking makes use of standard cooking utensils found in most kitchens, so you may already have what you need.

## Wooden Stirring Spoons

- Wooden utensils are great to use with nonstick cookware, as they are smooth, light on touch, and won't scratch the surface.

- Bamboo utensils are generally of higher quality and last forever if well main-tained. However, these days you can find a large variety of material choices at most kitchenware stores.

- Always clean and season your wooden utensils well and avoid putting them in the dishwasher.

## Spatulas

- Spatulas come in a wide range of sizes, both in handle length and face width.

- Spatulas with a longer face are best for flipping large firm food like omelets and Indian breads. A wider-faced spatula is best for lightly sautéing meats or vegetables.

- For use with nonstick cookware, it's best to opt for silicone spatulas since they are heatproof and won't scratch the surface of the pan.

# SPECIAL EQUIPMENT

## A few pieces of special equipment may be needed for cooking certain traditional recipes

Although the majority of Indian cooking can be successfully carried out with the simple tools available in most kitchens, there are a few recipes that may require some specialized equipment. Most of these recipes, however, are a step out of the ordinary, and you can always find simple alternatives to cater to them.

Before you fork over the extra cash to invest in these special pieces, I suggest considering how often you would actually use them. In most cases, cheaper and simpler alternatives can easily be found, and you may not need to buy any of them at all. If you decide to invest in them, I suggest doing a bit of research to find a piece that will best suit your needs.

### Pressure Cookers

- A pressure cooker is a sealed vessel that does not allow air or moisture to escape below a certain level of pressure. This enables the food to cook much faster.

- Pressure cookers are great for speeding up the cooking times of red meat and dried lentils or beans, as they can easily cut the time in half.

### Muslin Cloth

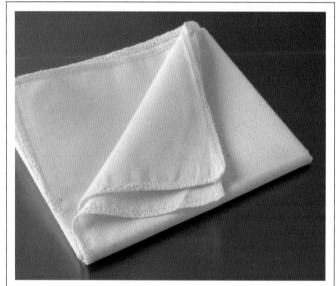

- A muslin cloth is mainly required to strain the excess moisture in yogurt. The cloth is filled with yogurt and the ends tied, then hung to enable excess water to seep through. What remains after a couple of hours is a thick, creamy yogurt.

- You will also find great use for a muslin cloth during the preparation of paneer, since the milk solids need to be drained through the mesh to rid them of any excess moisture.

4

However, with some special pieces like muslin cloth, there really isn't any good substitute for a fine one, and you will surely want to have one in your kitchen if the need arises.

## Spice Rack

- A spice rack is a great way to organize and store the spices that you have accumulated throughout the course of cooking various Indian foods.

- Depending on the amount of spices you use often, the size and shape of your spice rack can vary. A vertical carousel design is often a great way to save on counter space.

- Always keep the spices that you regularly use within arm's length so you can have quick and easy access to them as needed.

## Cheese Grater

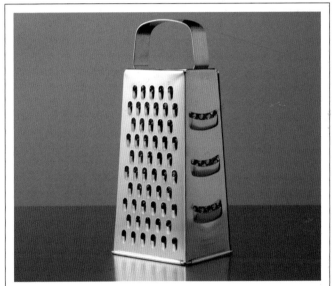

- A cheese grater is a great tool to use in the kitchen when you need to finely grate vegetables like cucumbers or beets.

- A box grater is often the preferred choice in most kitchens because of its ease in use and sturdiness.

- A cheese grater is also a great way to crumble paneer for use in recipes like parathas or scrambled paneer.

# SEEDS

## These spice seeds are often used to impart flavor by sautéing in hot oil

Spice seeds like cumin, mustard, and coriander are usually the first things added to hot oil to begin the cooking process. Sautéing these seeds help to infuse the flavors throughout the dish as well as give it body and texture. This process is known as tempering and is one of the main methods of adding flavor to a simple boiled dal recipe. Once the seeds start to sizzle and impart their aroma, the next ingredient is added.

In traditional Indian kitchens, whole spice seeds are bought in large quantities and are often dry roasted and pounded into a fine powder as needed. This way the flavors are always fresh, ensuring that the food tastes great. These days, with

### Cumin Seeds

- Cumin seeds are widely used in Indian cooking and are readily available at most local grocery stores.

- These seeds have a distinct pungent aroma and release flavor when heated.

- Whole cumin seeds are often dry roasted and finely ground to make cumin powder.

### Mustard Seeds

- Mustard seeds are more popular and widely used in the southern part of India.

- The black mustard seeds used in Indian cooking differ in taste from the yellow mustard seeds used to make the condiment. Although in some parts of India yellow mustard is used, black mustard seeds dominate in more mainstream Indian cooking.

- When selecting mustard seeds, look for ones that are either shiny black or dark gray.

the busy lives that we all lead, it is almost impossible to prepare a fresh batch of spices right before dinnertime. Hence, most households currently reach for pre-prepared spices.

Most of these spice seeds are readily available at regular grocery stores and can be bought in packs of varying weight. Always make sure to store them in a cool, dry place away from any direct heat to prevent them from losing flavor. This will ensure that they remain fresh for a longer time and impart their robust and fresh flavors.

You can also buy many of the common spice seeds in bulk assortments. This will allow you to purchase smaller quantities so that you can try them out and get used to their flavor without investing in large packs. It will also allow you to buy spices that you don't commonly use in your cooking in smaller amounts, as needed for a recipe.

## Coriander Seeds

- Coriander seeds impart a subtle smoky flavor and an added crunch when sautéed in hot oil.

- They are the seeds of the coriander plant and are readily available at most regular grocery stores.

- Coriander seeds release a slightly citrusy aroma when crushed and are mostly used in northern Indian cooking.

## Nigella Seeds

- Nigella seeds are commonly known as black onion seeds, or *kalonji* in Hindi.

- They can be found in the spice aisles of most grocery stores.

- Nigella seeds release a wonderful aroma when fried and impart a robust touch of flavor to a dish.

# WHOLE SPICES

These spices are generally added whole to a dish and release a wonderful aroma as they slowly cook

Whole spices are usually added to impart a depth of flavor into the recipe. They continue to infuse the dish throughout the entire cooking process. Whole spices are generally discarded when the dish is served, since accidentally biting into them can ruin the delicate balance of flavors on the palate.

These spices are a great way to add intense flavors to slow-simmering broths. It is always a good idea to bruise the spices a little before adding them to a dish to enable maximum release of flavor. Whole spices can also be dry roasted in a large nonstick pan and ground to a fine powder.

Keep your whole spices in a cool, dry place. Since they generally have a strong aroma, it is best to store them in

*Black Peppercorns*

- Whole black peppercorns add a much milder flavor while cooking compared to freshly ground pepper.

- Whole peppercorns are commonly added to slow-simmering curries along with other whole spices to infuse the dish with a blend of aromatic flavors.

*Cloves*

- Cloves impart a robust aroma and strong spicy flavor to a dish.

- The essential oils in cloves are often used for aromatherapy purposes.

- Because of their robust flavor, cloves are usually used in small amounts.

- Cloves are the main flavor enhancer in the spiced Indian tea known as chai.

separate spice jars so that the flavors remain distinct.

You can buy most of these whole spices in bulk assortments depending on how much you need. This will give you a chance to try them and get acquainted with the flavors before investing in a large pack.

## *Green Cardamom*

- Green cardamom has a slightly sweet aroma and taste. Though it is most commonly used to flavor Indian curries, it is also often found in Indian desserts.

- The green pods are generally lightly smashed to release the flavor, which is strongly concentrated within the seeds.

- The seeds of the cardamom are also added to chai while it brews.

## *Cinnamon Sticks*

- Cinnamon is a readily available, highly flavorful spice that is commonly used to season curries, soups, and sweets.

- It is actually the bark of a tree, and when added to curries, provides a woody, incense-like aroma.

# SPICE POWDERS
## No Indian kitchen is complete without these standard spices

The four classic spice powders—red chili, turmeric, coriander, and cumin—are among some of the most commonly used spices in Indian cooking. Though you may find these spices in the majority of Indian recipes, varying amounts and different methods of cooking are what create the distinct flavors of each dish.

These spices are readily available at regular grocery stores,

and if you have them on hand, more often than not a quick and simple curry is only a few minutes away. You can buy them either by weight in bulk or in the form of sealed packs of varying weights and sizes.

Traditionally, these spices are dry roasted in the whole form like seeds or sun dried chilies, and then ground to a fine powder. If you have the time, it may be a good idea to prepare

### Red Chili Powder

- Red chili powder is made by finely grinding dried red chilies. When shopping for this spice at a regular grocery store, you might want to look for it under the name cayenne.

- Red chili powders often vary in heat, depending on the kind of dried chili used.

- Be careful when adding it to your cooking, since too much heat can ruin the taste of a dish. Add it sparingly at first, making sure you are comfortable with the heat level.

### Turmeric Powder

- Turmeric powder is usually what gives the yellow tinge to Indian curries.

- Turmeric lacks a spicy flavor per se and has always been used in Indian cooking

more for its medicinal and ayurvedic properties.

- A little goes a long way with turmeric, and adding too much of it can give your dish a slightly bitter taste.

your own fresh batch of spice powders. This way, you can always be sure to have a fresh, robust flavor imparted into your cooking.

Once ground, store these spices in airtight glass jars. Always make sure to keep these spices in a cool, dry place away from direct heat. If stored well, they can stay fresh for a couple of months.

## Coriander Powder

- Coriander powder is made by dry roasting whole coriander seeds and finely grinding them.

- This powder gives a soft, subtle flavor to Indian food and is used in many recipes.

- To add maximum flavor and freshness to your Indian cooking, grind coriander seeds fresh as needed.

## Cumin Powder

- Cumin powder adds a soft, smoky flavor while cooking. It pairs perfectly with coriander powder and is often used in synchronization.

- This powder is readily available at most local grocery stores and will store well if kept in a cool, dry place.

# SEASONING SPICES

## These special spices are what makes Indian curries distinct from other Asian cuisines

Spice blends are a mix of various spices and seasonings that are brought together to create a new dimension of flavor. Traditionally, these spices were fresh ground right before use to ensure that the flavors remained robust in the dish.

Most spice blends vary in taste depending on the amount of individual spices used. Almost every authentic Indian kitchen has its own secret-recipe blend that it prides itself in.

Garam masala is one of the most common and popular spice blend used in Indian cooking. It usually consists of varying amounts of cumin, coriander, cloves, cardamom, cinnamon, and black pepper among other spices.

Chaat masala, another popular spice blend used mostly

*Garam Masala Powder*

- Garam masala is a robust blend of spices that includes cinnamon, cloves, cumin, peppercorns, and bay leaves, among a few others.

- The color and taste of store-bought garam masala often varies depending on the kinds of spices and amounts used.

- Garam masala can either be added during the cooking process or sprinkled on top of the dish after it is cooked to add an extra layer of flavor.

*Amchoor Powder*

- Amchoor powder is a dried mango powder that adds a strong, tangy flavor to a dish.

- Raw green mangoes are sun-dried and ground to make amchoor powder. It is generally added to dishes that require a tart flavor.

- Amchoor powder can be found at most ethnic stores. However, if you find it hard to find, you can substitute fresh lemon juice.

in the northern part of India, is usually made by grinding amchoor, dried ginger, black pepper, and coriander. It imparts a slight tang when added and is great sprinkled over fritters or potatoes.

## MAKE IT EASY

You can usually find these spices at any ethnic store, as well as at most regular grocery stores.

*Saffron*

- Saffron is one of the most expensive spices to be found. It usually comes in threads of red or deep orange and is derived from the dried stigma of a particular crocus.

- You will find saffron sold in tiny boxes, and usually not more than a pinch or two is needed to impart its aromatic flavor to a dish.

- When added to a dish, saffron leaves behind a trail of deep red color, and this is often what distinguishes the classic biryani from a simple pilaf.

### What is Curry?

- Curry is a gravy-based dish of either meat or vegetables.

- It can vary in style, color, and flavor depending on the region and kitchen it comes from.

- A curry mainly consists of three basic components: flavor base, feature ingredient, and flavor enhancers.

- A flavor base is the main ingredient that would dominate the flavor of the curry dish and could range anywhere from a simple blend of spices to coconut, yogurt, or tomatoes.

- The feature ingredient is the meat or vegetable that would carry the dish.

- Flavor enhancers can range anywhere from herbs, spices and condiments, or sauces.

# DRIED LEAVES

## These flavor enhancers add a dash of taste and aroma to any simple dish

Dried leaves generally impart a much deeper and more robust flavor to cooking compared to their fresh versions. In most cases a small amount of dried leaves will give you twice as much flavor as adding double the amount of their fresh counterpart.

Dried leaves store extremely well in the right conditions and stay fresh for a long period of time. Store dried leaves in airtight glass containers to prevent them from losing their fragrance.

You can find these leaves in regular grocery stores, often sold in sachets of varying weights. Don't be afraid to add them to your stews, soups, or curries for that extra burst of flavor.

### Dried Bay Leaves

- Dried bay leaves are often used to flavor rice curries and pilafs. They impart a mild aromatic taste.

- Always remember to discard the dried leaves before serving a dish, as biting into one will release a bitter taste.

### Dried Mint Leaves

- Dried mint leaves are frequently used in rich meat-based curries to infuse a delicate touch of flavor.

- Often sold in large packets, dried mint leaves usually have tiny stems attached. Because of the drying process, you can use the stems in cooking along with the leaves.

- To get maximum flavor, simply crush the dried leaves and stems between your fingers before adding them to the dish.

**Fresh versus Dried Herbs:** Fresh herbs will give you a burst of flavor and are best used as a garnish to complement a dish. Dried herbs impart a deeper flavor when used in the cooking process and intensify in taste.

When using dried herbs always remember that a little goes a long way as compared to its fresh alternative. Dried herbs are a great way of adding a particular flavor to a dish during colder months when fresh greens are less readily available.

## Dried Fenugreek Leaves

- Also known as kasoori methi, dried fenugreek leaves give that distinct flowery aroma to curries.

- It is usually added during the last few minutes of the cooking process to give the dish a new dimension of flavor.

- The kasoori methi is that sweet, subtle flavor that lingers on the palate in the classic Butter Chicken.

### Curry Leaves

- Curry leaves are most commonly used in cooking in south India.

- While most cooks prefer to use fresh leaves, it also works well when used in its dry form.

- Many Indian grocery stores sell fresh curry leaves in bulk. Use fresh leaves immediately and let the remaining leaves rest in the sun to dry, to prevent them from going rotten.

- Store dried leaves in an airtight glass jar and keep in a cool, dry place.

15

# LENTILS

## Lentils play an integral role in a traditional Indian meal

Lentils are basically legumes and have somewhat of a rich, nutty flavor. They are usually sold prepackaged in bags or boxes, but can also be bought in bulk. When storing lentils, it is best to keep them in large airtight containers in a cool place. Right next to where you store your pasta is probably also the best spot to display your lentil collection.

When shopping for lentils, it is important to note how much of an effort you are actually willing to spend in their cooking process. Lentils come in various sizes, shapes, and colors, each equipped with its own distinct flavor and different cooking time. Most of them can be cooked in similar ways, but don't let the differences in taste surprise you.

*Dried Red Lentils*

- Red masoor lentils are the type most commonly used in many homes.

- They take the shortest time to cook and require no presoaking whatsoever.

- This type of lentil is usually found in everyday meals and makes a quick go-to dish when you're running short on time.

*Dried Yellow Lentils*

- The toor dal is dull yellow in color and is often the base for many south Indian specialties like Sambhar.

- These lentils need to soak for a few hours before cooking and take longer to boil down to a soft edible center.

- A good way to overcome the long cooking process is to use a pressure cooker.

- On the other hand, yellow lentils are perfect for a slow cooker if you want to let a meal do its thing while you go about your business.

A typical Indian meal includes rice, a few rotis, a dal, and a vegetable, accompanied with some yogurt, pickle, and a light salad. When you don't have the time to go the whole mile, dals are best enjoyed with simple rice and a dash of pickle. In many Indian households, a different dal is cooked each day, accompanied with a complementing vegetable.

Dals are also used in many non-vegetarian preparations. Lentils are chock-full of proteins and are a great addition to a vegetarian diet. Add a handful to your stews and soups for that extra burst of nutrition. Lentils can easily take on varied flavors and add richness to your daily meals.

## *Dried Split-Pea Lentils*

- The chana dal, or split-pea lentil, has a deep yellow color and looks like half of a chickpea, only smaller in size.

- These lentils take the longest time to cook and are extremely compatible with both the pressure cooker and the slow cooker.

- They often take center stage in special dishes, and are a favorite to serve at dinner parties.

## *Dried Black Lentils*

- Being black in color and taking the shape of a tiny bean is probably what sets this dal apart from its various counterparts.

- Black lentils take fairly long to cook and need to be soaked overnight to soften. This lentil is the main ingredient in the classic Dal Makhani.

# FLOURS
## Indian cooking makes use of a wide range of flours and grains

Indian breads are made from various flours and grains and drastically differ in taste and texture from each other. Although whole wheat is most commonly used to make most kinds of Indian breads, you will also find interesting uses of millet, corn, and chickpea flour in Indian cuisine.

Always store your flours in airtight glass jars in a cool, dry place away from direct heat. For maximum freshness, practice buying flour in smaller quantities as opposed to oversize bags.

### Whole-Wheat Flour

- Whole-wheat flour is used to make the traditional Indian bread called roti and the stuffed version, paratha.

- A simple dough is made with water and a pinch of salt.

- The rolled-out dough is then cooked on a hot griddle.

### All-Purpose Flour

- All-purpose flour is generally used to make leavened yeast breads like naan.

- It is also popular for making pastry shells in recipes like samosas, where the pastry is stuffed with a potato filling and deep-fried until crisp.

## YELLOW ● LIGHT

Flours should be stored in a cool, dry place to keep them fresh for longer. When you open a large pack of any kind of flour, make sure to store it in an airtight container to prevent any moisture buildup, which can ruin its shelf life.

## GREEN ● LIGHT

Whole-wheat flour is most commonly used in Indian breads and can easily be used as a substitute in most recipes that call for white flour.

*Chickpea Flour*

*Semolina*

INDIAN MARKET BASKET

- Chickpea flour, also sold as besan at ethnic stores, is made by grinding dried roasted chickpeas into a fine powder.

- It is generally used to make vegetable fritters, or pakodas, in Indian cuisine.

- Chickpea flour is also commonly used in Indian kitchens as a thickening agent in the making of marinades for meats and kebabs.

- Semolina, also sold as sooji at most ethnic stores, is made from durum wheat and is often used in the manufacturing of pasta.

- It is a favorite in Indian cooking and is widely used as a breakfast item and for making the popular south Indian pancakes called dosas.

# COOKING STAPLES

## These cooking staples are must-haves in any Indian pantry

Indian cooking requires a few simple ingredients to make the food taste exotic and fresh. Pantry staples like basmati rice, coconut milk, and yogurt are widely used in Indian cooking and should be readily available in the pantry for use anytime they are required.

Always keep your pantry well equipped with these staples to make dinnertime quick and simple. With these items stocked in your pantry, you can make most of the recipes, provided you have the main ingredients at hand.

### Basmati Rice

- Basmati is a flavorful long-grain Indian rice that is readily available at most regular grocery stores.

- Basmati gives off a slightly sweet aroma while it cooks, and when prepared properly, each grain remains separate and does not stick together.

- Basmati is generally sold in large bags of 5 to 10 pounds each, but can also be found in smaller, more economical packaging as well as in bulk.

### Canned Coconut Milk

- Canned coconut milk is readily available at most grocery stores, usually in the baking or international foods aisle.

- These days many stores also carry a light version of coconut milk, which has less fat content and works equally well as a substitute for regular coconut milk in any recipe.

20

Once you have these staples and are confident about using them, then go a step further and try out a few more that may be new to you. Slowly, but surely, you'll build your own collection of ingredients and spices that you're fond of and know would enable you to cook meals that you like.

When it comes to cooking simple Indian food, you only need to be familiar with a few spices and the flavors that go with them. As a self-starter, it's very easy to get lost in the wide selection of ingredients used in Indian cooking. True, they may seem intimidating at first, but then as you go along and acquaint yourself with the robust flavors they have to offer, you can't help but get excited at the prospect of shopping and stocking your pantry with some of your favorites.

## Plain Yogurt

- Plain yogurt is commonly used in Indian curries to give them a smooth, creamy texture.

- Natural Greek yogurt most resembles the yogurt traditionally used in India; however, low-fat or nonfat yogurt works equally well in most recipes.

## Tamarind

- Tamarind is widely used in Indian recipes as a souring agent.

- While traditional recipes often call for the use of tamarind juice, which is made by soaking dried tamarind in hot water and releasing its pulp, you can easily use store-bought tamarind concentrate as a substitute.

# FRESH HERBS

These fresh herbs are used to garnish as well as flavor Indian food

Fresh herbs like cilantro and mint are regularly used in Indian cooking as a garnish. They also add great visual appeal to the dish along with a fresh burst of flavor. In addition, fresh herbs are commonly blended with spices to create rich and robust chutneys.

Always store fresh herbs wrapped in damp paper towels in the fridge to make them last longer. When picking herbs like cilantro, be sure to look for leaves that are tender and deep green in color. This indicates that the leaves are fresh and have maximum flavor.

*Cilantro*

- Cilantro sprigs are regularly used as a fresh garnish on many Indian dishes.
- The leaves are tender and give out a sweet, fresh aroma when chopped.

*Mint Leaves*

- Mint leaves are often used in Indian salads and curries to add a robust flavor.
- While fresh mint leaves are usually used as a garnish on many dishes, dried mint leaves are also commonly used to flavor a dish during the cooking process.

Fresh herbs like cilantro and mint that are mainly used as a garnish should be added right before the food is to be served. Doing so will prevent the herbs from wilting or browning in the warmth of the dish and losing their robust flavor.

## Curry Leaves

- Curry leaves are usually added to hot oil at the beginning of the cooking process to give a slightly aromatic flavor to the dish.

- Curry leaves are commonly used in southern Indian cooking and can be readily found at most grocery stores.

### Freezing Herbs:

- Freezing is a quick and easy way to preserve the flavor of fresh herbs.

- Finely chop fresh herbs and freeze by filling an ice cube tray with 1 tablespoon measurements.

- Frozen herbs will retain their fresh flavor for a couple of months and can be used in the same proportions as that of their fresh counterparts.

- They are perfect to use in cold winter months over soups or stews.

INDIAN MARKET BASKET

# PANEER

## This soft Indian cheese is a favorite of vegetarians

Paneer is a soft mild cheese that is made by adding lemon/lime juice to hot milk to curdle it, and then strained to get rid of any excess moisture.

To make fresh paneer at home, heat 2 quarts of whole milk until it starts to boil. Slowly add 2–3 tablespoons of fresh lime juice, just enough so that the milk starts to curdle. Turn off the heat and let it rest for a couple of minutes. Carefully pour the contents into a muslin cloth placed over a large bowl, and bring the ends together, tying it into a tight knot.

Hang the bundle over the kitchen sink to enable the whey to drip away. After about an hour, when all the moisture has leaked out, the paneer will form into a firm ball. Slice this into cubes, and use as directed.

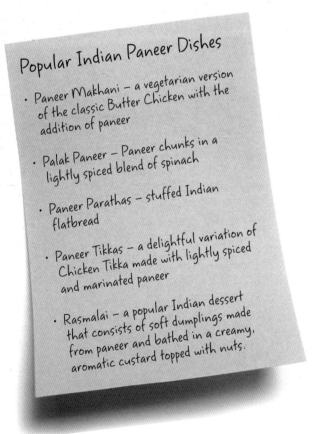

### Popular Indian Paneer Dishes

- Paneer Makhani – a vegetarian version of the classic Butter Chicken with the addition of paneer

- Palak Paneer – Paneer chunks in a lightly spiced blend of spinach

- Paneer Parathas – stuffed Indian flatbread

- Paneer Tikkas – a delightful variation of Chicken Tikka made with lightly spiced and marinated paneer

- Rasmalai – a popular Indian dessert that consists of soft dumplings made from paneer and bathed in a creamy, aromatic custard topped with nuts.

*Paneer*

- Ready-made paneer is available at most ethnic stores and can be bought in large blocks.

- Paneer is very mild tasting and easily takes on any flavor added to it.

- Because it does not disintegrate and melt at high temperatures, it is a great option to use on the grill.

## Crumbled Paneer

## Tofu and Cottage Cheese

- Cubed paneer is mainly used in curries, stir-fries, and on the grill. They work really well when cut into 1-inch chunks since they maintain their shape and do not break or melt in the cooking process.

- Crumbled paneer is best suited for use in recipes as a filling, like in parathas or samosas. It will not melt at high heat and can blend well with spices and other ingredients to take on the flavors.

- Firm tofu has a slightly similar texture to that of paneer and can be used as a substitute if you find it hard to get your hands on a block of paneer at the store.

- Cottage cheese is also quite similar in taste and texture to paneer, except that it may contain more moisture. This can be a good substitute to use where crumbled paneer is called for, but you might want to wring out any of the excess moisture first.

# POTATO SAMOSAS

## Re-create this popular Indian street food by using frozen puff-pastry sheets

Samosas are one of the most popular snacks in India and are commonly sold by street vendors. Traditionally, they are deep-fried and enjoyed as a snack either with a cup of tea or a side of spicy chutney in the evenings. These are bound to disappear fast, so make sure you save yourself a piece or two before handing them out.

By using ready-made frozen puff-pastry sheets, you can avoid the deep-frying process altogether and, in turn, make this recipe more doable on a busy weeknight. For a quick dinner option, serve the samosas with a large side salad. As an alternative, you can add any leftover vegetables you may have to the filling. *Yield: Serves 4–6*

**Ingredients:**

1 teaspoon cumin seeds

1 tablespoon vegetable oil

1 small onion, finely chopped

1–2 green chilies, finely chopped

2 garlic cloves, minced

1 teaspoon turmeric powder

1 teaspoon garam masala powder

2–3 medium potatoes, boiled and cut into small cubes

Salt, to taste

2 (10 x 10 inch) sheets frozen puff pastry, cut into 9 equal squares each

*Potato Samosas*

- Sauté cumin seeds in hot oil until they start to sizzle. Add onions, green chilies, and garlic and fry until onions are soft and transparent.

- Stir in turmeric and garam masala; fry 1 minute. Add potato cubes; sauté until spices mix well with pota-toes. Season with salt. Set aside.

- Add about a tablespoon of potato filling to the center of a pastry square and seal edges together to form a triangle. Repeat for all squares. Bake in a 375ºF preheated oven 20–25 min-utes until golden brown.

*Make the Filling*

- Since the potatoes are used to make the filling, cut them into as small cubes as possible.

- The filling should be completely cooled before it is used, so you can easily

make it a day ahead of time and store it in the fridge.

- Adding frozen peas or carrots to the potato mixture will increase the nutritional value of this dish.

*Use of Puff-Pastry Sheets*

- You can make an extra batch of samosas and freeze them for later. These can be placed into the oven straight from the freezer without thawing.

- Using spring roll or wonton wrappers instead of puff pastry sheets can be a nice variation; however, they will need to be deep-fried.

APPETIZERS

# JALAPEÑO PANEER POPPERS
## Inspired by a favorite at bars and pubs, this snack blends East and West

I got the idea for this recipe one day when I was cleaning out my fridge in preparation for my weekly grocery shopping. I came across a couple of jalapeño peppers that desperately called for my attention. Being an ardent fan of the pub classic cream cheese–filled jalapeño poppers, I decided to give them a try at home, but the lack of cream cheese in my fridge made me improvise with the half block of paneer that I did have.

Since these tend to be a huge hit with almost everyone I've served them to, I generally prepare a big batch and freeze them once they're coated with the bread crumbs. Then I either deep-fry them or bake them in the oven when my guests are about to arrive. *Yield: Serves 4–6*

## Ingredients:

3 garlic cloves, minced

1 tablespoon vegetable oil

200 grams paneer, grated

1/4 teaspoon red chili powder

1/2 teaspoon coriander powder

1/2 teaspoon cumin powder

1/2 teaspoon garam masala powder

2 tablespoons tomato paste

Salt, to taste

10 jalapeños, halved and deseeded

2 eggs, beaten

1 1/2 cups bread crumbs

Oil, for deep-frying

*Jalapeño Paneer Poppers*

- Sauté garlic in hot oil until fragrant. Add paneer, spices, and tomato paste and fry 5–6 minutes until everything is well blended.

- Season with salt, and mix to blend well.

- Pack each jalapeño half tightly with the paneer filling. Dip into beaten egg and then bread crumbs to coat on all sides.

- Deep-fry in hot oil until golden and crisp.

## *Make the Filling*

- The paneer must be slightly warm to the touch while filling the jalapeños so that it can be packed in tightly.

- If the paneer was made ahead of time and cooled, simply heat it in the microwave for a minute or two before filling the jalapeños.

## *Using Jalapeños*

- Make sure you pick jalapeños that are firm and plump so that they can hold a good amount of the filling.

- To deseed jalapeños, cut them in half lengthwise and, with a paring knife, scrape out the seeds and ribs. Since this is what gives jalapeños their spiciness, the heat level will be drastically cut down.

- Serve this dish immediately, as it tastes best when warm and crisp. Any leftovers can be easily reheated in the oven.

APPETIZERS

# MASALA POPCORN CHICKEN
## Spice up run-of-the-mill chicken nuggets with a fresh new blend of flavors

Chicken nuggets are one of the most popular go-to dinner options for families with fussy eaters. The next time you're chopping up chicken and coating it with bread crumbs for your meal, try this version instead. The blend of spices is just enough to tickle your taste buds without setting them on fire. This is also a good way to introduce kids to different flavors without actually forcing them to try a new dish.

Personally, I prefer using cuts of dark meat since they remain moist and tender on the inside while being crisp on the outside. However, if you're not a fan of dark meat, lean chicken breast pieces work well, too. *Yield: Serves 4–6*

### Ingredients:

4 boneless chicken thighs

$1/4$ teaspoon red chili powder

$1/2$ teaspoon coriander powder

$1/4$ teaspoon cumin powder

$1/2$ teaspoon garam masala powder

$1/2$ teaspoon salt

2 eggs, beaten

$1 1/2$ cups bread crumbs

Oil for deep-frying

*Masala Popcorn Chicken*

- Pat the chicken thighs dry and cut them into bite-size pieces.

- Mix the chicken pieces with the spices and salt. Marinate in the fridge for at least an hour.

- Create an assembly line by lining up chicken next to the beaten eggs and the bread crumbs, each in a wide dish.

- Dip each piece of chicken into the beaten eggs and then the bread crumbs to coat well. Deep-fry in hot oil until golden brown and crisp.

30

## Marinate the Chicken

## Deep-Fry the Chicken

- The longer the chicken marinates in the spices, the better it will absorb the flavors. For best results, leave it in the fridge for 2–3 hours.

- To make this recipe kid-friendly, omit the chili powder and use chicken breasts instead of thighs.

- For a healthier alternative, bake in a preheated 425°F oven for 15–20 minutes until cooked through.

- To test if the oil is ready for frying, throw a pinch of bread crumbs into the pot. If they start to immediately sizzle and float to the top, your oil is hot and ready.

- If, however, they blacken immediately, then the oil is overheated. Take it off the heat and allow to cool.

- Make sure the oil is not overheated; if it is, the chicken will burn on the outside without completely cooking through.

- To prepare an extra batch for later use, freeze the chicken after coating it.

APPETIZERS

31

# COCONUT-CRUSTED SHRIMP

## An intensely flavorful twist on the classic breaded shrimp

In the southern part of India, where the coast makes it possible to have seafood and coconuts in abundance, it is no surprise that these two ingredients dominate the region's cuisine. I've always enjoyed the combination of shrimp and coconut in curries, and decided to take that classic pairing a step further.

The sweetness of the coconut comes through perfectly, and paired with tender shrimp is a delight to the palate. I like to hit it with a dash of fresh lemon juice as it comes out of the oil to brighten up the flavors even more. Enjoy this shrimp dipped into some minty mango chutney for a wonderful burst of tropical flavor. *Yield: Serves 3–4*

### Ingredients:

12–15 large shrimp, peeled and deveined

1/2 teaspoon red chili powder

1 teaspoon coriander powder

1/4 teaspoon salt

Oil, for deep-frying

1 egg, beaten

1 cup unsweetened coconut flakes

2–3 lemon wedges

*Coconut-Crusted Shrimp*

- Pat shrimp dry and mix with spices and salt to coat well. Let sit 10–15 minutes to marinate.

- In the meantime, heat enough oil in a large pot to deep-fry.

- Dip each shrimp in beaten egg to coat, then dredge in coconut flakes. Fry shrimp in hot oil in batches 1–2 minutes until golden and cooked through.

- Sprinkle with fresh lemon juice and serve with an extra wedge of lemon.

# · · · · RECIPE VARIATION · · · ·

**Coconut Shrimp and Mango Wraps:** Place 2–3 coconut-crusted shrimp on a warm flour tortilla, and top with lettuce and mango slices. Sprinkle with chopped peanuts and roll into a tight wrap.

*Prepare the Shrimp*

- To devein shrimp, run a paring knife down the length of the shrimp to expose the vein, and gently pull it out.

- Pre-cleaned shrimp can be found in the frozen section of most grocery stores. To use frozen shrimp, let them thaw in a bowl of cold water for about half an hour.

- The shrimp should be dry before mixing them with the spices; otherwise, they won't coat properly.

*Deep-Fry the Shrimp*

- Be sure to remove the shrimp from the hot oil as soon as they turn golden; otherwise, the coconut will burn and give a bitter taste.

- As an alternative, use panko or bread crumbs instead of coconut.

- To prepare an extra batch for later use, freeze the shrimp after coating them with the coconut.

APPETIZERS

# CUMIN SMASHED POTATOES

## With a crisp exterior and soft interior, these baby potatoes are perfect as a light snack

Potatoes are as popular with Indians as pasta is with Italians. It is often hard to come across a menu of Indian delicacies without potatoes included in at least one of them. Since potatoes are quite bland on their own, they can really carry the intense flavor of Indian spices. I generally prefer using yellow baby potatoes since they contain much less starch.

However, red and white baby or fingerling potatoes would also work very well.

These potatoes pair perfectly with roast chicken or lamb, as well as make a wonderful addition to any tapas menu. I like to top each potato with a dollop of thick cucumber raita before serving. *Yield: Serves 3–4*

### Ingredients:

12 baby new potatoes

$1/4$ teaspoon red chili powder

$1/2$ teaspoon coriander powder

1 teaspoon cumin powder

$1/2$ teaspoon salt

2 tablespoons vegetable oil

Juice of half a lemon

*Cumin Smashed Potatoes*

- Boil potatoes with skins on until tender, about 20–25 minutes. Smash each potato with the back of a spoon to flatten slightly.

- Mix spices and salt in a small bowl. Sprinkle generously over each potato.

- Place potatoes on a greased baking sheet and lightly drizzle with oil. Bake in a preheated 425°F oven 15–20 minutes until potatoes begin to brown and are crisp.

- Squeeze lemon juice over the potatoes and serve warm.

*Smash the Potatoes*

*Season the Potatoes*

- Smashing the potatoes while they are still warm will help flatten them more easily.

- Instead of a spoon, you can use a potato masher or a flat wooden ladle to flatten the potatoes.

- Make sure not to press too hard, or else the potatoes will break and fall apart.

- Remember to season the potatoes liberally before baking them; otherwise, they will end up tasting a bit bland.

- For different flavor options, use grill seasoning or other flavored salts.

- You can use a spray-on vegetable oil to ensure the potatoes are coated evenly.

APPETIZERS

# STUFFED MUSHROOM CUPS

## Marinated mushrooms topped with spiced sautéed onions make for a delightful combination of texture and flavor

Until recently, mushrooms weren't readily available at local markets in India. It is for this reason that mushrooms are often thought of as an exotic ingredient used mostly in high-end restaurants. A popular pick on many restaurant menus would be Mushroom Tikkas, delicately spiced and grilled to perfection.

In this recipe, I wanted to elevate the simplicity of the marinated mushrooms by topping them with a mix of sweet and sour flavors. These mushrooms are a perfect finger food that can be passed around a party, and are amazing served either warm or at room temperature. *Yield: Serves 3–4*

### Ingredients:

1 teaspoon cumin seeds

3 garlic cloves, minced

1 tablespoon vegetable oil

1 cup finely chopped onions

1/4 teaspoon red chili powder

1/2 teaspoon garam masala powder

Salt, to taste

2 tablespoons minced fresh cilantro

12 cremini mushrooms, stems removed

1 cup plain yogurt, beaten until smooth

1 teaspoon coriander powder

1 teaspoon cumin powder

Salt, to taste

2 tablespoons fresh lemon juice

*Stuffed Mushroom Cups*

- Sauté cumin seeds and garlic in hot oil until they sizzle. Add onions, chili powder, garam masala, and salt and fry until onions soften and are lightly brown. Mix in cilantro and set aside to cool.

- Meanwhile, marinate mushrooms in yogurt, coriander and cumin powders, salt, and lemon juice for about half an hour.

- Take mushrooms out of the marinade, discarding any excess. Stuff with 2 teaspoons of onion topping.

- Bake in a preheated 425°F oven 15–20 minutes until tops start to brown.

**Cheesy Stuffed Mushrooms:** Add ¼ teaspoon each of red chili powder, coriander powder, and cumin powder to 1 cup shredded mozzarella cheese and mix well. Top each marinated mushroom with a tablespoon of spiced cheese and bake in a preheated 325°F oven for 15–20 minutes until cheese melts.

**Stuffed Mushroom Salad:** Serve warm stuffed mushrooms over a bed of mixed greens such as baby spinach, arugula, and romaine lettuce. Add sliced tomatoes and walnuts, sprinkle with fresh lemon juice, and serve as a hearty salad for lunch.

*Make the Topping*

- You can make the onion topping ahead of time and store it in the fridge.

- The oil used to cook the onions is enough to help brown the topping when it bakes, so you don't need to spray the tops before placing the mushrooms in the oven.

*Prepare the Mushrooms*

- Pick mushrooms that are wide enough to hold at least 1 tablespoon of the filling.

- Marinating the mushrooms in yogurt will give them an added flavor and tenderize them.

- Do not let the mushrooms sit in the marinade for more than half an hour, as they can start to turn soggy.

APPETIZERS

# CHICKPEA PATTIES

## An Indianized version of the Middle Eastern falafel

Beans and lentils are widely used in Indian cuisine, mainly because a large part of the vegetarian population gets its protein intake from them. You will often find beans or lentils served with a meal, or added to snacks to increase their nutritional value.

Growing up in the Middle East, I enjoyed my fair share of fresh-made falafels, but always wondered if you could switch spices to incorporate Indian flavors. This version of mine is fairly quick and simple to make, and it is perfect when you need to whip up something at a moment's notice. On busy weekdays, I like to make large burger-size patties and serve them between toasted buns with a salad and chutney on the side. *Yield: Serves 3–4*

### Ingredients:

2 cups canned chickpeas

1 small onion

2 garlic cloves, peeled

1 green chili

2 tablespoons chopped fresh cilantro

1 teaspoon cumin powder

1 teaspoon coriander powder

$1/4$ teaspoon red chili powder

$1/2$ teaspoon garam masala powder

2 tablespoons fresh lemon juice

2 tablespoons all-purpose flour

$1/4$ teaspoon salt

Oil, for frying

*Chickpea Patties*

- Drain and thoroughly rinse canned chickpeas to rid of any excess salt. Drain the rinsed chickpeas well to remove any trace of moisture.

- Place all the ingredients, except the oil, in a food processor and blend until smooth.

- Divide into 12 roughly equal parts and form into patties.

- Heat the oil in a nonstick pan and shallow-fry patties in batches, about 3–4 minutes on each side until brown and crisp.

If you use dried chickpeas, soak a cup of them overnight in a large bowl of room-temperature water. The next morning, drain the water and rinse the chickpeas thoroughly. Add the chickpeas to a large pot filled with water, and boil 30–35 minutes until tender.

## • • • • RECIPE VARIATION • • • •

**Chickpea Patty Pockets:** Cut warm pitas in half to open them up. Fill the pita pockets with 1–2 chickpea patties, slices of tomato, and lettuce. Beat ½ cup plain yogurt with ¼ teaspoon each of red chili powder and cumin powder, a pinch of salt, and 2 tablespoons lemon juice. Sprinkle 2–3 tablespoons of the yogurt sauce into the pita pockets and serve as a quick, hearty lunch.

### Blend until Smooth

- The chickpeas should be drained properly since adding water to the mixture can make it soggy and difficult to form into patties.

- If using dried chickpeas, soak a cup overnight and then boil until tender. Let them cool completely before running them through the food processor.

### Form and Fry the Patties

- If the mixture is too sticky to form into patties right away, refrigerate for about an hour to firm it up a bit.

- Remember not to overcrowd the pan while frying; if you do, the patties will not have enough heat to brown properly.

- Be careful when flipping the patties while frying to prevent them from breaking.

# TUNA CUTLETS
## Fresh, tangy flavors come together in these crisp fried fish cakes

These tuna cutlets are a much healthier way to enjoy the goodness of fish cakes without the addition of cream or mayonnaise. Potatoes are used to bind the ingredients together and add body and texture to the cutlets. The lemon juice highlights the freshness of the cilantro, and the spices add a subtle burst of flavor. Although I generally prefer using canned tuna for this recipe, you can easily substitute canned crab meat.

Either enjoy the cutlets as burgers, or make them into smaller sizes to serve as appetizers. I love serving this for lunch on warm summer days with a large salad on the side. *Yield: Serves 2–3*

## Ingredients:

1 large potato

1 can tuna, packed in water

1 small onion, finely chopped

1 green chili, finely chopped

2 tablespoons minced fresh cilantro

1 tablespoon fresh lemon juice

1 teaspoon coriander powder

1/4 teaspoon amchoor powder

1/4 teaspoon salt

Oil, for frying

1 egg, beaten

*Tuna Cutlets*

- Boil the potato until tender and set aside to cool. Mash it to a smooth paste.

- Mix all the ingredients except the oil and egg and form into 6 patties.

- Heat enough oil to coat a nonstick frying pan.

- Dip each patty into the beaten egg to coat well. Fry 4–5 minutes on each side until brown.

**Spicy Tuna Melts:** Mix the tuna with the onions, spices, cilantro, and salt. Spread over thick slices of French bread and top with shredded mozzarella cheese. Bake in a preheated 375°F oven for 10–15 minutes until bread turns crisp and cheese melts.

**ZOOM**

Do not use canned tuna packed in oil for the cutlets. The oil will interfere with the texture of the cutlets and prevent them from binding well. Always use tuna packed in water, and be sure to drain it well to get rid of excess moisture.

## Mix the Ingredients Well

- Make sure the ingredients are mixed well so that there is equal distribution of spices, tuna, and potatoes in each cutlet.

- Do not use canned tuna packed in oil, as it will make the cutlets oily and hard to form into patties.

- You can form the patties ahead of time and store them wrapped in plastic in the fridge.

## Fry the Cutlets

- Always use enough oil to coat the pan well to ensure that the cutlets are crisp on all sides.

- To get an even crispier outside layer, you can coat the cutlets in bread crumbs after dipping them in the beaten egg.

**APPETIZERS**

# SPICED TOMATO SOUP
## Jazz up this winter favorite to tantalize your taste buds

Tomato soup is one of the most common winter comfort foods. On most Indian restaurant menus, you can find a spicy, creamy version of tomato soup called Tamatar Shorba. This is usually made with a blend of aromatic spices and a dash of cream to thicken it.

My version brings together a subtle hint of spice and a mild aroma from dried fenugreek leaves. Sautéing the cumin seeds and garlic brings a sweeter, tender touch to the sweet stewed tomatoes, and blending the soup until smooth helps balance and meld these flavors. This soup makes a perfect first course with a few crisp croutons sprinkled on top. For a light, quick lunch, pair this soup with a grilled cheese sandwich or a hearty salad. *Yield: Serves 2–3*

### Ingredients:

1 teaspoon cumin seeds

3 garlic cloves, minced

1 teaspoon oil

4 large tomatoes, roughly chopped

1/4 teaspoon red chili powder

3 cups water

1 teaspoon dried fenugreek leaves

Salt, to taste

*Spiced Tomato Soup*

- Sauté cumin seeds and garlic in hot oil in a deep pot, until they start to sizzle.

- Add chopped tomatoes and chili powder and fry for a few minutes until tomatoes begin to pulp.

- Add water and let it come to a boil. Stir in dried fenugreek leaves and let simmer 10–15 minutes.

- Using a hand blender, blend soup until smooth. Season with salt and serve immediately.

42

**Tomato Vegetable Soup:** Add ½ cup each of frozen corn, peas, and carrots to the blended soup. Let it simmer for 10–15 minutes until vegetables are warmed through, and serve piping hot with grilled cheese sandwiches for a light and balanced lunch.

Use diced canned tomatoes to quicken the cooking time. Canned tomatoes found in grocery stores often have spices or seasonings added to them, so be sure to pick a brand without any added flavors, as they would alter the flavor of the dish.

### Fry the Tomatoes

- Always use fresh, ripe, plump tomatoes, as they will generally have a more robust flavor.

- If your tomatoes are not very fresh and sweet, you can add a pinch of sugar while frying to bump up the flavor.

### Blend the Soup

- Use a deep pot while operating the hand blender to avoid splattering the soup.

- If you don't have a hand blender, let the soup cool to room temperature before running it through a blender or food processor.

- Reheat until it starts to bubble, and serve.

SOUPS

# COCONUT LENTIL SOUP

## A creamy, hearty soup to warm up a cold evening

A blend of lentils and vegetables in a rich coconut broth, this soup is my simplified version of the classic mulligatawny. The yellow lentils boil to mush fairly quickly and add a smooth, meaty texture to the soup. Although this soup is fairly mild, the curry leaves add a subtle burst of flavor.

Due to the rich texture of this soup, it makes a great lunch when paired with a side salad. I like to make a few extra helpings of the soup and freeze it for a later use. Be sure to store it in an airtight freezer-friendly container. The soup will stay fresh for a couple of weeks in the freezer. *Yield: Serves 3–4*

## Ingredients:

1 teaspoon cumin seeds

4–5 fresh curry leaves

3 garlic cloves, minced

1 teaspoon oil

$^1/_2$ cup yellow lentils

2 cups water

1 cup coconut milk

$^1/_4$ teaspoon turmeric powder

$^1/_2$ teaspoon red chili powder

1 teaspoon coriander powder

Salt, to taste

1 tablespoon lemon juice

*Coconut Lentil Soup*

- Sauté cumin seeds, curry leaves, and garlic in hot oil in a deep pot, until they start to sizzle.

- Slowly stir in lentils and water and cook 20–25 minutes until lentils are tender and break easily between your fingers.

- Stir in coconut milk, spices, and salt. Cover and simmer the soup 10–15 minutes to blend and intensify the flavors.

- Sprinkle with fresh lemon juice and serve immediately.

To cut down on the cooking time, you can use canned lentils instead of dried. Generally, canned lentils found at most grocery stores tend to be of the brown variety used mainly in French cooking. Although brown lentils will alter the taste and texture of this recipe, they can work quite well. Make sure you drain and rinse the lentils thoroughly to eliminate any of the excess salt and preservatives.

Store-bought dried lentils usually have tiny stones in them, so be sure to pick through the lentils thoroughly to get rid of any unwanted additives. To make picking through a large amount of lentils much easier, spread them out on a tray and slowly examine them.

## Cook the Lentils

- Always boil lentils over low heat, as they tend to froth. You can slowly skim the top with a ladle to remove the froth.

- To avoid excessive froth, rinse the lentils thoroughly before boiling.

- Lentils should always be completely immersed in water while boiling, so check them regularly to make sure that the water does not dry up.

## Prepare the Coconut Milk

- Coconut milk is readily available in grocery stores in cans. These days you can also usually find light versions of coconut milk, which would also work really well in this recipe.

- Shake the can thoroughly before pouring the coconut milk since it tends to separate.

# CHICKPEA SOUP

## Chickpeas are simmered with spices in a stock and blended into a smooth, creamy soup

I created this recipe one evening when I was in the mood for something simple and soothing. As I looked through my fridge and pantry, all I found useful was a can of chickpeas and a carton of vegetable broth. I used simple spices to season the broth and simmered the chickpeas in it for a while. As I began to blend the contents into a smooth, textured soup,

it suddenly occurred to me that if I left it the way it was, I could enjoy it with some rice as a fairly thinned-down curry.

Serve this soup piping hot with some crusty bread on the side. If you are planning a multicourse meal, I would suggest pairing this soup with a chicken curry, sautéed potatoes, and some rice. *Yield: Serves 3–4*

**Ingredients:**

2 cups canned chickpeas

2 garlic cloves, minced

1 medium onion, finely chopped

1 teaspoon oil

$1/2$ teaspoon red chili powder

1 teaspoon cumin powder

1 teaspoon coriander powder

2 tablespoons tomato paste

3 cups vegetable stock

Salt, to taste

*Chickpea Soup*

- Drain the canned chickpeas and rinse thoroughly.

- Sauté garlic and onions in hot oil in a deep pot, until the onions are soft and lightly browned. Add spices, tomato paste, and chickpeas and fry to coat mixture well.

- Stir in vegetable stock and simmer 10–15 minutes.

- Remove from heat and use an immersion blender to blend soup until smooth. Season with salt and serve immediately.

To make a simple Indian version of vegetable stock, add 3–4 garlic cloves, a 1-inch piece of ginger, 1 large chopped onion, 1 large chopped tomato, and 2–3 diced carrots to 3 cups of water. Add 5–6 white peppercorns, 3–4 whole green cardamoms, 2–3 whole cloves, and salt to taste. Bring to a full boil and then simmer for about an hour over low heat. Drain the stock once cooled and use immediately, or store it in the freezer for later use.

## ···· RECIPE VARIATION ····

**Red and Black Bean Soup:** You can substitute red kidney beans or black beans for the chickpeas in this recipe. Either bean would work really well since their texture is fairly similar to the chickpea's, but the flavors are different.

*Drain the Chickpeas*

*Prepare the Stock*

- Always drain and thoroughly rinse canned chickpeas to get rid of any added salt or preservatives.

- Two 15-ounce cans will generally give you 3 cups of chickpeas.

- If using dried chickpeas, soak them overnight in a large bowl of water and rinse thoroughly before boiling them in a large pot.

- It may take anywhere from 20 to 30 minutes to tenderize the beans while boiling, depending on their shape and size.

- Use premade stock to save on time. For extra added flavor, you can substitute chicken stock for vegetable stock.

- If you find yourself without any ready-made stock on hand and have no time to

prepare a fresh batch of your own, simply use plain water for the recipe.

- Just be sure to simmer the soup an extra 15–20 minutes over low heat to intensify the flavors.

SOUPS

# SPICED YOGURT SOUP

## This simple yogurt soup is thickened with chickpea flour and spiced with fennel seeds

This recipe is strongly inspired by a yogurt curry called kadhi, popular in the Punjab region of India. Traditionally, kadhi is slightly thick in consistency and includes tiny fritters made of onions and spinach. As much as I love the unique flavors carried in kadhi, I find it a hassle to make a batch of fritters to go along with it, not to mention the curry's unhealthy aspect.

Thinning kadhi down and serving it as a soup enables you to enjoy the warm flavors of this dish without the effort required to make it the traditional way. I love to have this soup before a simple meal of roti and dal. *Yield: Serves 3–4*

### Ingredients:

2 tablespoons cup chickpea flour

1 cup plain yogurt

2 cups water

1 teaspoon oil

$1/2$ teaspoon cumin seeds

$1/4$ teaspoon fennel seeds

1 small onion, finely sliced

$1/2$ teaspoon red chili powder

$1/4$ teaspoon turmeric powder

Salt, to taste

*Spiced Yogurt Soup*

- Whisk the flour, yogurt, and water together until there are no lumps. Set aside.

- Heat oil in a deep pan and sauté cumin and fennel seeds. Once they start to sizzle, add onions and fry until lightly browned. Add spices and fry for a few more seconds.

- Stir in yogurt water, season with salt, and bring to a full boil. Remove from heat and serve immediately.

Chickpea flour, also sold as besan at ethnic grocery stores, is made by grounding dried roasted chickpeas into a fine powder. It is generally used to make vegetable fritters, or pakodas, in Indian cuisine. Chickpea flour is also commonly used in Indian kitchens as a thickening agent in the making of marinades for meats and kebabs.

## YELLOW LIGHT

To spice up this dish the traditional Indian way, add 2–3 whole dried red chilies to the hot oil before sautéing the cumin and fennel seeds. Let the chilies simmer in the oil for a few seconds until they begin to turn a deeper red. The chilies can start to burn fairly quickly, so avoid this by making sure the heat is not too high and keeping a watchful eye on them.

### Prepare the Yogurt Mixture

- Be sure to thoroughly whisk the yogurt and flour into the water to eliminate any lumps.

- While working with ingredients, remember that chickpea flour can be found at many local grocery stores and almost all ethnic stores and can be kept fresh in a tight canister in a cool, dark place.

### Boil the Soup

- The chickpea flour will tend to thicken the soup, so add extra water if needed to thin it.

- The final consistency that you're looking for is somewhat slightly thicker than that of a clear soup— almost like the consistency of a crepe batter.

# CHICKPEA & POTATO SALAD

## Switch up your everyday potato salad with a delightful, healthy version

Boiled chickpeas mixed with onions, chilies, and spices are often sold by street vendors and enjoyed as a quick snack in northern India. Commonly referred to as chana chaat, these are usually eaten with a spicy chutney and fresh green chilies on top. Here, I've added cubed potatoes and just enough seasoning to lightly flavor the dish. The key is to use fresh

cilantro, which adds a whole new dimension of flavor.

You can serve this either as a first course or alongside a meal consisting of a spicy, meaty curry. I also like to add chopped tomatoes and turn the dish into a quick, filling lunch or light dinner. *Yield: Serves 3–4*

### Ingredients:

2 cups canned chickpeas

1 medium potato

2 tablespoons minced fresh cilantro

1/4 teaspoon red chili powder

1/2 teaspoon garam masala powder

2 tablespoons fresh lemon juice

Salt, to taste

*Chickpea and Potato Salad*

- Drain canned chickpeas and rinse thoroughly to get rid of any excess salt and preservatives. Drain thoroughly.

- Boil the potato and once cooled, cut into bite-size cubes.

- Mix all the ingredients in a bowl, combining well. Let sit in the refrigerator 10–15 minutes to allow the flavors to blend. Serve chilled.

Add finely chopped fresh green chilies to this recipe. Street vendors in India usually have bowlfuls of chopped chilies from which they take tablespoonfuls and liberally add them at the customer's discretion. If you're still looking to turn up the heat but don't want to set your palate on fire, try using fresh green jalapeños instead of chilies. Although they are fairly hot, they are a touch milder.

## • • • • RECIPE VARIATION • • • •

**Mixed Bean Salad:** Substitute the canned chickpeas with canned mixed beans and add 1 large chopped tomato instead of the potato. Sprinkle with the spices and lemon juice and serve on a bed of fresh, crisp lettuce.

### Rinse and Drain Chickpeas

- Remember to rinse canned chickpeas thoroughly; otherwise, the salt content could affect the taste of the salad.

- This salad can easily be prepared ahead of time and stored in the fridge for up to an hour. Just make sure to leave out the cilantro and add it right before serving.

### Finely Chop Cilantro

- If you plan on making this dish a day in advance, do not chop and add the cilantro until a few minutes before serving to avoid discoloration.

- Fresh cilantro are best enjoyed as soon as they are chopped to ensure maximum flavor.

# SPICY CORN SALAD
## A jazzed-up corn salsa with a hint of spice

I threw this recipe together on a whim one evening in a feeble attempt to feed some unexpected guests. Little did I know it would soon become one of the most requested items from my kitchen.

The dish literally takes minutes to bring together, but what I've realized with time is that if you let it sit for a couple of extra minutes, the flavors will intensify. The sourness of the chaat masala pairs perfectly with the sweetness of the corn. Add some heat to kick the flavor up a couple more notches. To be honest, I've hardly ever served this dish on its own. It usually accompanies grilled chicken or fish, or even better, a big bowl of tortilla chips. *Yield: Serves 3–4*

## Ingredients:

2 cups frozen corn kernels

2 tablespoons minced onion

1 jalapeño, deseeded and minced

2 tablespoons finely chopped fresh cilantro

1/4 teaspoon red chili powder

1 teaspoon cumin powder

1 teaspoon chaat masala powder

2 tablespoons fresh lemon juice

Salt, to taste

*Spicy Corn Salad*

- Place the frozen corn in a large bowl and let it thaw to room temperature. If you're in a hurry, you can run the frozen corn under warm water in a colander to thaw it out in a flash. Drain well.

- Mix all the ingredients in a bowl to combine well. Let the salad rest in the refrigerator 10–15 minutes to allow the flavors to blend. Serve chilled.

Chaat masala is a spice mix commonly used in northern Indian cooking and typically consists of amchoor powder, cumin, black salt, and coriander, among a few other spices. It generally has a pungent smell and tastes sour and slightly salty. You can find it at most ethnic stores sold in boxed packs as well as many regular grocery stores.

## GREEN ● LIGHT

Serve this with a side of simple grilled chicken breast marinated in a dash of olive oil with some lemon juice, cumin powder, coriander powder, salt, and pepper. This will make for a filling lunch or a quick, light dinner. You can also mix chopped grilled chicken with the corn salsa to make a more heartier salad to be enjoyed on its own.

### Deseeding Jalapeños

- To deseed a jalapeño, cut off the top and split it in half lengthwise.

- With a paring knife, scrape out the ribs and any leftover seeds. Since this is

what gives the jalapeño its spiciness, the heat level will be drastically cut down.

- Rinse the jalapeños thoroughly to wash out any excess heat.

### Mixing the Ingredients

- To make sure that the spices mix well and coat the corn properly, use a large ladle to fold the ingredients a few times to incorporate all the flavors.

- The flavors here will intensify as the salad sits.

# SPICED CABBAGE SLAW

## Serve this slaw at your next barbecue, and your burgers will never taste the same again

I've always enjoyed a good helping of coleslaw alongside my burger, but could never avoid the guilt that comes with it. Coleslaws are generally packed with a good helping of mayonnaise, and this makes it a forbidden dish for most calorie-conscious diners. By substituting yogurt for the mayonnaise and adding a pinch of Indian spices, I can now eat as much slaw as I want and know that it is also good for me.

Be careful serving this slaw outdoors, though. As with any fresh yogurt-based dish, it should be served chilled and kept away from warm temperatures to prevent the yogurt from cracking. For a quick lunch, I like to make wraps with grilled chicken topped with the slaw. *Yield: Serves 3–4*

## Ingredients:

³/₄ cup plain yogurt

2 cups finely shredded cabbage

¹/₂ cup finely shredded carrot

¹/₂ teaspoon cumin powder

¹/₄ teaspoon red chili powder

¹/₄ teaspoon garam masala powder

1 tablespoon fresh lemon juice

1 tablespoon minced fresh mint leaves

Salt, to taste

*Spiced Cabbage Slaw*

- Beat the yogurt in a large bowl until smooth.

- Slowly fold in the shredded cabbage and carrot and coat well.

- Add the spices, lemon juice, mint leaves, and salt and mix well to combine. Let sit in the fridge 10–15 minutes and serve chilled.

## MAKE IT EASY

If you're pressed for time and need to hasten the preparation of this already simple recipe, feel free to use a ready-made store-bought coleslaw mix. You can find this at most grocery stores in the salad aisle beside the chopped greens. Coleslaw mix usually includes shredded green and red cabbage and carrots.

## • • • • RECIPE VARIATION • • • •

**Red Cabbage Slaw:** Trade the shredded green cabbage for a red cabbage and bump up the flavor by adding 2 tablespoons of finely chopped cilantro. The red cabbage has a more intense flavor and can support the fresh cilantro nicely.

*Shred Cabbage and Carrots*

- You can shred cabbage easily with a food processor or a mandolin.

- If you're pressed for time, use prepackaged coleslaw mix.

- For added crunch and a burst of color, throw in ¼ cup of shredded beets.

*Beat the Yogurt*

- Beating the yogurt until smooth gives the slaw a creamy texture.

- Do not store this salad for too long, as the yogurt can

dry up and the vegetables will start to turn mushy. It is best enjoyed freshly made while the vegetables still retain their crunch.

# MINT & CUCUMBER SALAD

## Mint and yogurt combine to create a flavorful dressing for fresh cucumbers

I created this recipe as a modern version of the classic cucumber raita. Instead of grating the cucumbers and blending them with the yogurt, I thought it would look more appetizing if I topped sliced cucumbers with a spiced yogurt dressing to make a fancier-looking salad. The mint adds a burst of freshness to the dressing and is really the star of this dish.

Raita is usually served with a traditional Indian meal, since the coolness of the yogurt generally helps to mitigate the heat from the spices in the food. This salad, however, would be equally great served as a first course or with soup and sandwiches for lunch. *Yield: Serves 1–2*

### Ingredients:

2 tablespoons plain yogurt

1 teaspoon olive oil

1 tablespoon fresh lemon juice

$1/4$ teaspoon cumin powder

$1/4$ teaspoon coriander powder

Salt, to taste

1 cup thinly sliced cucumber

2 tablespoons minced fresh mint

*Mint and Cucumber Salad*

- Make a smooth dressing with the yogurt, olive oil, lemon juice, spices, and salt.

- Layer sliced cucumbers neatly on a plate and pour dressing evenly on top.

- Garnish with chopped fresh mint.

# ···· RECIPE VARIATIONS ····

**Tomato and Onion Salad:** Cut 2 medium tomatoes into wedges and thinly slice 1 medium white onion. Layer tomatoes and onions on a flat dish and top with yogurt dressing and chopped mint. Serve this salad with a side of grilled salmon for a quick, hearty lunch.

**Citrus Yogurt Dressing:** Change this recipe by altering the dressing. Substitute the plain yogurt for an lemon-flavored yogurt and leave out the mint leaves. Instead, garnish the salad with a sprinkle of lemon zest.

## *Make the Dressing*

- This simple, quick dressing can be whipped up a couple of minutes before serving.

- Since yogurt is the main ingredient, make the dressing fresh before serving since it won't keep well stored for long.

## *Slice and Layer the Cucumbers*

- Because this is a very simple salad, presentation is key.

- Layer the cucumbers on a circular plate, overlapping each other, and drizzle the dressing over them in a spiral for a dramatic effect.

- You can also throw in a few thin slices of fresh tomato for added color and flavor.

# CLASSIC CHICKEN CURRY

## A favorite in many Indian homes, chicken curry can be prepared in a variety of ways

Curries can be a quick go-to solution when you don't have much time to fuss over dinner and are best enjoyed with a side of plain white rice or warm Indian bread called roti. Whip up a quick salad and make it a complete meal.

Using boneless chicken in the curry ensures a quick cooking time. However, if you decide to make a pot of chicken curry on a Sunday afternoon and have a few extra minutes to spare, use bone-in cut-up pieces of chicken instead. It may take an extra 10 to 15 minutes but will give the dish a much richer flavor. To prevent the spices from burning easily, use a heavy-bottomed pan. *Yield: Serves 3–4*

## Ingredients:

1 cinnamon stick

3-4 cardamom pods, bruised

3-4 whole cloves

4-5 whole black peppercorns

2 tablespoons vegetable oil

1 large onion, finely chopped

2-3 green chilies, finely chopped

1 tablespoon ginger-garlic paste

$1/2$ teaspoon red chili powder

$1/4$ teaspoon turmeric powder

1 teaspoon coriander powder

$1/4$ teaspoon cumin powder

$1/4$ teaspoon garam masala powder

2 medium tomatoes, finely chopped

Salt, to taste

$1/2$ cup plain yogurt, beaten

2 large boneless chicken breasts, diced into 1-inch cubes

2 tablespoons chopped fresh cilantro for garnish

*Classic Chicken Curry*

- Sauté the first 4 spices in the oil until they sizzle.

- Add onions and green chilies and fry 3–5 minutes. Add ginger-garlic paste and sauté 2 minutes.

- Add the next 5 spices and fry for 1 minute. Mix in

chopped tomatoes and salt and cook until tomatoes release oil around the sides of the pan. Stir in yogurt.

- Add chicken and a cup of water, and cook covered 10–15 minutes over medium-low heat. Garnish with cilantro.

**Light Chicken Curry:** To make a much lighter version of this curry, simply omit the yogurt and bump up the flavor by adding a dash of fresh-squeezed lemon juice before serving. Serve over a bowl of plain basmati rice with a big salad on the side.

**Vegetarian Yogurt Curry:** For a vegetarian version, instead of chicken, add chunks of vegetables like cauliflower, carrots, and potatoes. Dice the potatoes into bite-size cubes and let the curry simmer 10–15 minutes longer to ensure that the potatoes are tender and cooked through.

*Make Ginger-Garlic Paste*

*Prepare the Yogurt*

- To make ginger-garlic paste, simply peel and place equal amounts of ginger and garlic into a food processor and blend until smooth. Add a dash of water if necessary.

- When stored in a clean jar with a tight lid, this can stay fresh in the fridge for up to 2 weeks.

- To save on future cooking time, fill each section of an ice-cube tray with a tablespoon of ginger-garlic paste and store it in the freezer. Use within 4–6 weeks.

- Beating yogurt to a smooth consistency before adding it to a warm dish prevents it from separating due to heat. This will also help bring out a creamy curry base.

- Always be sure to use plain yogurt for cooking. To cut down on the fat content, feel free to use a fat-free or low-fat version. They work just as well.

# CREAMY CHICKEN WITH RAISINS
## A quick, modern twist on the classic Butter Chicken

Butter Chicken, also known as Chicken Makhani at many Indian restaurants, undoubtedly is one of the most popular curries in Indian cuisine. As much as I enjoy a delicious bowl of it with warm naan, I can't help but question the amount of time it must take to cook, not to mention the liberal addition of butter and cream.

In my version of the recipe, I tried to re-create this classic dish by reducing the amount of cream used and throwing in a couple of raisins to bump up its overall sweetness. The boneless chicken drastically cuts down on the cooking time, and the pureed tomatoes help the curry come together without the need to simmer for a long time. *Yield: Serves 3–4*

### Ingredients:

2 large boneless chicken breasts, diced into 1-inch cubes

2 tablespoons vegetable oil

1 tablespoon minced garlic

¹/₂ teaspoon red chili powder

¹/₄ teaspoon turmeric powder

1 teaspoon coriander powder

2 large tomatoes, pureed

1 cup water

¹/₄ cup raisins

Salt, to taste

2 tablespoons cream

*Creamy Chicken with Raisins*

- Sauté chicken pieces in hot oil until slightly browned. Add garlic and spices and fry for a few seconds to coat the chicken.

- Stir in pureed tomatoes, water, and raisins and let the mixture come to a boil.

- Season with salt and add cream. Cook covered for a 20–25 minutes until chicken is cooked through.

## • • • • • RECIPE VARIATION • • • •

**Creamy Mushroom Curry:** To make a delightful vegetarian version of this recipe, replace the chicken with 3 cups of white button mushrooms cut into quarters. Before adding the pureed tomatoes, sauté the mushrooms with the garlic and spices until all their moisture dries up and they begin to brown. Serve with warm naan or a side of saffron pilaf.

## • • • • • • GREEN ● LIGHT • • • • • • • •

Chicken breasts are generally used in this recipe, but you can definitely use boneless chicken thighs or a mix of both. This curry freezes extremely well, and you can make an extra batch to save in the freezer for a later date. Be sure to let the curry cool completely to room temperature, then store it in wide freezer-friendly containers. When you're ready to serve a frozen batch of the curry, defrost it in the fridge overnight, then heat it in the microwave.

### *Prepare the Chicken*

- When making this recipe, using chopped boneless chicken breasts drastically shortens the cooking time.

- You can also use boneless chicken thighs if you prefer dark meat.

- Dice chicken into 1-inch cubes.

### *Puree the Tomatoes*

- To puree tomatoes, quarter and place them in a food processor or blender, and blend until smooth.

- If you find that the tomatoes are a bit firm and don't have enough juice to blend into a smooth puree, add a tablespoon or two of water to help get it started.

# CILANTRO CHICKEN
## Commonly known as Indian Green Curry, this dish is a breeze to make

Green chicken curry in India is mostly made with a combination of various greens and herbs. Usually, that would mean a longer preparation time, which is why this dish would mostly be served on special occasions. By sticking to one aromatic, flavorful herb, the cooking time is cut down enough so that this dish can be featured on a regular weeknight.

Cilantro is regularly used as a garnish on many Indian curries, but using it as a base for the curry itself brings out a whole new side of this popular herb. Once you have all the ingredients prepped and ready to go, this dish is quick and easy to prepare. *Yield: Serves 3–4*

**Ingredients:**

2 tablespoons vegetable oil

1 small onion, finely chopped

2 bay leaves

1 cinnamon stick

1 tablespoon ginger-garlic paste

1/2 teaspoon red chili powder

1/4 teaspoon turmeric powder

1 teaspoon cumin powder

1/2 teaspoon garam masala powder

2 large boneless chicken breasts, diced into 1-inch cubes

2 tablespoons tomato paste

2 cups chopped fresh cilantro, pureed

1 cup water

Salt, to taste

*Cilantro Chicken*

- Heat oil in a deep nonstick pan and fry onions with bay leaves and cinnamon until onions start to lightly brown.

- Add ginger-garlic paste and spice powders and fry a few seconds until fragrant. Add chicken pieces and mix well with spices.

- Stir in tomato paste, coriander puree, and water and cook covered for a few minutes until chicken is cooked through. Season with salt and serve warm.

## • • • • RECIPE VARIATION • • • •

**Spinach Chicken:** You can easily make a much more nutritious version of this curry by substituting the cilantro with some spinach. Both fresh and frozen spinach would work well. If you intend to use frozen spinach, however, you will need to defrost and drain it completely before pureeing it to a fine paste.

Cilantro is widely used in Indian cooking, both as a garnish and as an integral flavor base in a dish. When picking fresh cilantro, look for a bunch that smells fresh and is tender and bright green. Discard leaves that are browning around the edges, since those will lack in flavor. In most chutneys and marinades where cilantro is meant to be the dominant flavor, even the tender stems are used.

## *Make Ginger-Garlic Paste*

- To make ginger-garlic paste, simply peel and place equal amounts of ginger and garlic into a food processor and blend until smooth. Add a dash of water if necessary.

- When stored in a clean jar with a tight lid, this can often stay fresh in the fridge for up to 2 weeks.

- To save on future cooking time, fill each section of an ice-cube tray with a tablespoon of ginger-garlic paste and store it in the freezer. Use within 4–6 weeks.

## *Prepare the Cilantro Puree*

- Always use the freshest cilantro you can find to get maximum flavor for this dish.

- Put chopped cilantro and ¼ cup water in a blender or food processor and blend to puree until smooth.

# ALMOND CHICKEN CURRY

## A quick and easy version of the classic Chicken Korma

Chicken Korma is a mild, aromatic, creamy curry dish that has its origins in ancient Mughlai cuisine. You can often find it served at weddings or other special occasions. Its wonderful flavor comes from blending a bunch of spices along with a mix of nuts and cream.

When I set out to re-create a much more doable version of this classic, I knew I had to find ways to introduce flavor without the long cooking process. The blend of spices I chose to mix into this recipe are those that can stand up to provide maximum flavor as well as be readily available. I also switched the cream for a dash of yogurt to cut down on the fat content. Although this recipe is a far cry from the traditional, it can certainly match up to it in taste. *Yield: Serves 3–4*

## Ingredients:

2 tablespoons vegetable oil

1 medium onion, finely chopped

1 tablespoon minced garlic

1/2 teaspoon red chili powder

1/4 teaspoon turmeric powder

1 teaspoon coriander powder

1/2 teaspoon garam masala powder

1/4 cup ground almonds

2 large boneless chicken breasts, diced into 1-inch cubes

2 tablespoons tomato paste

1 cup plain yogurt, beaten

Salt, to taste

Pinch of dried fenugreek leaves

*Almond Chicken Curry*

- Heat oil in a deep nonstick pan and fry onions and garlic until soft and fragrant.

- Add spices and ground almonds and fry for a few seconds, being careful not to let it burn. Add chicken and sauté for a few minutes until lightly browned.

- Stir in tomato paste and yogurt and cook covered for 20–25 minutes until chicken is done.

- Season with salt and sprinkle dried fenugreek leaves. Cook covered for another 10 minutes and serve warm.

## GREEN ● LIGHT

Nuts are widely used in Indian cooking, most commonly in rich curries as a thickening agent. Adding ground nuts to a curry will help thicken its texture and give it a creamy, smooth consistency without adding cream. The ground almonds give this curry a slight sweetness without over-powering the other flavors.

**ZOOM**

Since this is a fairly mild-tasting curry, you can bump up the level of heat by adding chopped fresh chilies to the pan along with the chicken. The flavor of the green chilies will intensify as they simmer in the curry and turn up the spice level drastically. If you really want to spice it up, leave the seeds in the chilies.

### *Grind Almonds*

- To grind whole almonds, simply run a couple of handfuls through a spice grinder until finely powdered.

- Adding ground nuts to curries helps thicken them as well as give them a creamy consistency without adding any extra cream.

- To change this recipe a bit, use ground cashews instead of almonds.

### *Stir in the Yogurt*

- Make sure you stir the yogurt while adding it to the hot pan to thoroughly blend the spices and ground almonds into it.

- If the curry seems too thick or starts to dry up, add a couple tablespoons of water to get the desired consistency.

- This dish is best served piping hot with a side of freshly made naan.

# SAUTÉED CHICKEN WITH POTATOES
## Another version of the classic chicken curry

In India, chicken curries vary from kitchen to kitchen, with every family swearing they make the best one. Ingredients differ depending on the region the family is from, the climate they live in, and most importantly, the ingredients that grow in abundance around them.

This version of chicken curry is adapted from the state of Punjab, in the northern part of India. Since meat was sometimes quite costly to serve as the main meal for a large family, people started to mix in pantry staples like potatoes to stretch the recipe to feed more for less. This dish is more of a drier version of the regular curry and is best enjoyed with warm roti, the traditional Indian bread. *Yield: Serves 3–4*

## Ingredients:

2 tablespoons vegetable oil

1 large onion, sliced

1 tablespoon minced garlic

1 large potato, peeled and cubed

2 large boneless chicken breasts, sliced into thin strips

1/2 teaspoon red chili powder

1/4 teaspoon turmeric powder

1 teaspoon coriander powder

1/2 teaspoon amchoor powder

1 large green pepper, sliced into strips

Salt, to taste

*Sautéed Chicken with Potatoes*

- Heat oil in a nonstick wok and fry onions and garlic until soft and fragrant.

- Add potatoes and stir-fry for a few minutes until they start to brown along the sides and are partially cooked through.

- Mix in chicken, spices, and pepper and cook until chicken and potatoes are completely cooked through, about 20–25 minutes, stirring occasionally.

- Season with salt and cook for another 4–5 minutes.

### Cube the Potatoes

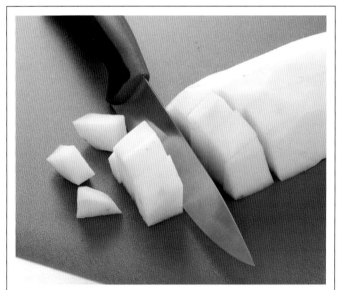

- To ensure that the potatoes cook quickly and evenly, cut them into small, bite-size cubes of roughly the same size.

- You can soak the chopped potatoes in a bowl of cold water for a few minutes to get rid of the starch.

### Slice the Chicken

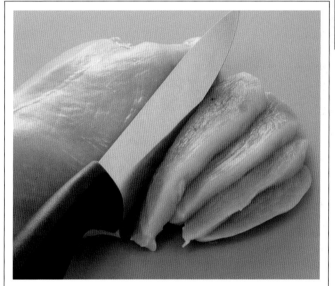

- Cut the chicken breasts into vertical strips and then slice each strip at an angle to get even, thin slices.

- You can substitute chicken breasts with thighs if you prefer a darker cut of meat.

# GINGER CHICKEN

## An aromatic chicken dish that will tickle your taste buds

Ginger is known for its pungency and can take a dish to a whole new level with its flavor alone. Cooking it with yogurt, however, can cut that pungency and, in turn, leave only a delicate inkling of its taste. I re-created this recipe from a version I once had at a dinner party a long time ago.

I like to make this dish on cold winter nights when the body yearns for something warm and comforting. Although the spice level is not too high, the undertones of ginger provide that much-needed depth in a winter curry. Serve it with an aromatic pilaf and some raita on the side. *Yield: Serves 3–4*

**Ingredients:**

2 tablespoons vegetable oil

2 dried red chilies

4 chicken thighs, cut into bite-size pieces

1 tablespoon minced ginger

1/4 teaspoon turmeric powder

1/2 teaspoon red chili powder

1 teaspoon coriander powder

1 teaspoon garam masala powder

1/2 cup plain yogurt, beaten

Salt, to taste

*Ginger Chicken*

- Heat the oil in a nonstick wok and add the red chilies. Once they start to sizzle, add the chicken, ginger, and spices and fry for a few minutes until chicken lightly browns, about 10–12 minutes.

- Stir in the yogurt, season with salt, and cook covered for a few minutes until the chicken is completely cooked through, around 15–20 minutes.

Fresh ginger is an aromatic, pungent spice that is widely used in Indian cooking. Ginger freezes wonderfully and you can pop any leftovers into the freezer, stored in a sealed bag, to keep it for a longer time. When you're ready to add it to your cooking, simply grate the ginger, skin and all, into the dish. The flavor will remain fresh and pungent, even after it has been frozen for a couple of weeks.

## • • • • RECIPE VARIATION • • • •

**Ginger Fish:** You can easily make a seafood version of this recipe by substituting the chicken with a firm white-fish like tilapia, haddock, or halibut, or even shrimp. Simply follow the steps in this recipe, omitting the chicken, of course, and add the fish or shrimp as soon as you've added the yogurt. Squeeze a dash of fresh lemon juice on top right before serving.

*Mince the Ginger*

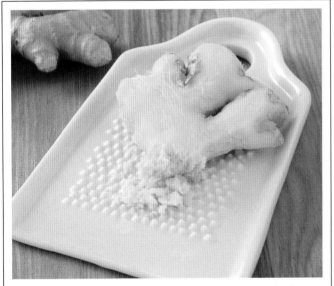

*Add the Spices*

- To make mincing a breeze, store fresh stubs of ginger in the freezer and simply grate one when needed.

- Storing ginger in the freezer keeps it fresh for a long time, and you'll always have it on hand to use.

- Be sure to sprinkle the spices evenly over the chicken and stir immediately to mix well.

- Remember not to fry the spices for too long. They can easily burn, which will give the dish a bitter taste.

# MINCED LAMB WITH PEAS

## Sweet peas combined with aromatic spices take ground lamb to a whole new level

Keema Matar is one of the most popular dishes with ground meat in Indian cuisine. Although it is common in most Indian homes, I haven't quite found it to be a regular at fancy Indian restaurants. A wide range of whole spices is used to add maximum flavor to ground lamb. Although lamb is often used in this recipe, you can definitely substitute lean ground chicken or turkey for a much lighter version.

Ground meat is a wonderful way to feed a large crowd on a low budget, and combined with frozen peas, this recipe is a definite winner at any potluck. This dish is best when served with warm roti or naan, and can be easily frozen for later use. *Yield: Serves 3–4*

## Ingredients:

1 teaspoon cumin seeds

3–4 whole green cardamoms

1 cinnamon stick

1–2 dried bay leaves

7–8 whole black peppercorns

2 tablespoons vegetable oil

1 large onion, finely chopped

1 pound lean ground lamb

2 medium tomatoes, finely chopped

$1/2$ teaspoon red chili powder

$1/2$ teaspoon cumin powder

1 teaspoon coriander powder

$1/2$ teaspoon garam masala powder

1 cup frozen green peas

$1/2$ cup water

Pinch of salt

*Minced Lamb with Peas*

- Sauté cumin seeds and whole spices in hot oil until they start to sizzle. Add onions and lamb and fry until lightly browned.

- Stir in tomatoes and spice powders and cook until tomatoes soften and begin to pulp.

- Add peas, water, and salt and cook covered 15–20 minutes until it all comes together and meat is completely cooked.

70

**Minced Meat Loaves:** Slice a baguette halfway lengthwise to open it up without breaking. Hollow out the baguette by removing its center flesh, making sure to leave a little around the edges. Fill with the minced lamb and close as firmly as possible. Wrap in foil and bake in a preheated 375ºF oven 10–12 minutes until the bread crisps. Slice into thick chunks and serve.

You can substitute the lamb with lean ground chicken or turkey for a much lighter fare. While browning the minced meat, be sure to sauté it well until all the moisture dries up and the meat begins to firm. Continue to break the meat with the back of your spoon to prevent any lumps from forming. Once the moisture is gone and the meat is well mixed with the onions, you can add the tomatoes and spices and continue the cooking process.

## Brown the Lamb

- Make sure to break up the meat while frying to avoid any clumps.

- Continue to fry the minced meat along with the onions until all the moisture has dried up and the meat is well blended with the onions.

## Stir in the Peas

- Continue to stir the meat while adding the peas so that they will mix well.

- When using frozen peas, remember to add them when the dish is just about done since they hardly need any time to soften.

GROUND MEAT

# MINCED LAMB & POTATO CURRY
## Meat and potatoes combine in an exotic new twist

Ground lamb and potato curry is one of those comfort foods that are a favorite in most Indian homes. As with many classic curries, each kitchen comes with its own special version of the recipe. My version includes adding yogurt to the curry to form a smooth, creamy consistency. The curry is then simmered over low heat to allow the sweet flavors of the cinnamon and bay leaves to infuse and blend into it.

This dish is best enjoyed with a side of warm naan and good company. I love to invite a couple of close friends over on a Friday night and serve this right from the pot. Everyone helps themselves, and I can be left to enjoy the wonderful conversation. *Yield: Serves 3–4*

## Ingredients:

- 1 cinnamon stick
- 1–2 dried bay leaves
- 2 tablespoons vegetable oil
- 1 large onion, finely chopped
- 1 pound lean ground lamb
- 2 medium tomatoes, finely chopped
- 1/4 teaspoon turmeric powder
- 1/2 teaspoon red chili powder
- 1 teaspoon coriander powder
- 1/2 teaspoon garam masala powder
- 1/2 cup plain yogurt, beaten
- 1 large potato, cubed
- 1 cup water
- Salt, to taste

*Minced Lamb and Potato Curry*

- Sauté cinnamon and bay leaves in hot oil until they start to sizzle. Add onion and lamb and fry until lightly browned.

- Stir in tomatoes and spice powders and cook until tomatoes soften and begin to pulp.

- Mix in yogurt, potatoes, water, and salt. Simmer covered 20–25 minutes until meat is completely cooked and potatoes are tender.

# • • • • RECIPE VARIATIONS • • • •

**Add Frozen Peas and Carrots:** You can add a cup of frozen peas and carrots to this dish to bump up its nutritional value. Simply stir in the peas and carrots once the potatoes are tender, and simmer for an extra 5–10 minutes to cook through. If using fresh carrots, chop them into bite-size pieces and add them halfway through the cooking process once the potatoes are partly done.

**Ground Chicken or Turkey:** You can substitute the ground lamb with lean ground chicken or turkey for a much lighter version. Using chicken or turkey will also lower the cooking time, since they tend to brown and cook through much quicker. While browning the meat, be sure to fry it well until all the moisture evaporates.

## *Prepare the Potatoes*

- Chop the potatoes into bite-size pieces to lessen the cooking time.

- To remove excess starch, soak the chopped potatoes in a bowl of cold water for

15–20 minutes, then rinse thoroughly.

- As an alternative, use baby new potatoes cut into halves.

## *Simmer the Curry*

- Let the curry simmer covered for a few minutes to allow all the flavors to blend in.

- The yogurt will thicken the curry a bit, so add extra water if you want more gravy.

# MEATBALL CURRY
## Chicken meatballs are simmered in a flavorful rich curry

Koftas, or the Indian version of meatballs, are made in different ways depending on the spices and seasoning used in them. For this recipe, I chose to let the meatballs cook in the curry itself, thereby infusing them with a well-rounded flavor. Doing this also helps to drastically cut down the cooking time. Most traditional versions would require you to first cook the meatballs by lightly frying them over low heat, and then adding them to a simmering curry. Serve this curry with a flavorful pilaf and some raita on the side. If you make an extra batch of meatballs, you can bake them in the oven and serve them with mild chutney as an appetizer. *Yield: Serves 3–4*

## Ingredients:

1 pound lean ground chicken

3 tablespoons minced onion

3 tablespoons minced fresh cilantro

1 tablespoon bread crumbs

1/2 teaspoon salt

1/2 teaspoon red chili powder

1 teaspoon garam masala powder

1 teaspoon cumin seeds

1 large onion, finely chopped

1 teaspoon minced ginger

1 teaspoon minced garlic

2 tablespoons vegetable oil

2 medium tomatoes, finely chopped

1/2 teaspoon red chili powder

1/2 teaspoon cumin powder

1 teaspoon coriander powder

2 cups water

Salt, to taste

*Meatball Curry*

- Mix the first 7 ingredients and form into 24 tiny meatballs. Set aside.

- Sauté cumin seeds, onions, ginger, and garlic in hot oil until onions start to brown and become tender.

- Add tomatoes, remaining spice powders, water, and salt and let it simmer for 10–12 minutes.

- Slowly add the meatballs and let it simmer covered for 15–20 minutes until the meatballs are completely cooked through.

**Spiced Meatball Wraps:** Make meatballs as directed and bake them on a greased baking sheet in a preheated 375°F oven for 15–20 minutes. Turn meatballs at least once in the middle of the cooking process to brown evenly on all sides. When done, roll them into warm flour tortillas with chopped lettuce, tomatoes, and cucumbers. Serve with mango chutney.

## GREEN ● LIGHT

To freeze extra meatballs for later use, spread the uncooked meatballs out on a greased baking sheet and pop it in the freezer. Once the meatballs are frozen, you can seal them in a freezer bag and store them in the freezer for up to 3 weeks. To use frozen meatballs, pop them unthawed into the curry or an oven, depending on how you plan to use them, and let them cook through.

## *Make the Meatballs*

- Be sure to mix the spices and ground meat well so that the flavors are completely blended through.
- Form golf-ball–size meatballs, dipping your fingers in water while shaping them to prevent the meat from sticking to your hands.

## *Simmer the Meatballs*

- Add the meatballs to the curry slowly to prevent splashing.
- Simmer the curry over low heat to enable the meatballs to completely cook through.

GROUND MEAT

# SPICY HERBED BURGERS

## Fresh cilantro and mild spices add a wonderful twist to everyday burgers

Burgers are a wonderful way to introduce people to new flavors. You can use any kind of meat you fancy, throw in a mix of spices and seasonings, and you'll have a winning combination. Since I have yet to come across someone who does not enjoy a good, juicy burger done perfectly on a hot grill, this recipe is sure to please guests at your next barbecue.

The cilantro adds a fresh contrast to the flavors of cumin and coriander. I love to serve these with an array of chutneys and yogurt dips to let my guests dress up their burger as they so please. You can also stuff a burger into a pita pocket and top with fresh lettuce and tomatoes for a quick lunch on the go. *Yield: Serves 3–4*

## Ingredients:

1 pound lean ground lamb

1 small onion, finely chopped

1 tablespoon minced ginger

1 tablespoon minced garlic

1 teaspoon minced green chilies

2 tablespoons minced fresh cilantro

1 teaspoon cumin powder

1 teaspoon coriander powder

1/4 teaspoon garam masala powder

1 tablespoon vegetable oil

1 egg, beaten

1/4 cup bread crumbs

*Spicy Herbed Burgers*

- Mix all the ingredients until well blended. Divide into 6 equal parts and form into burgers.

- Place burgers on a greased baking sheet and bake in a preheated 425ºF oven for about 20 minutes, flipping after 10 minutes, until cooked through.

Sometimes, when I make these burgers for a bunch of my spice-loving friends, I'll add a tablespoon of finely chopped green chilies or jalapeño along with the spices. It is very important to remember that since they are added fresh and are not precooked, the heat level will be drastically high. You can always remove the seeds, however, to cut down on the heat.

**Cocktail Meatballs:** Beat 1 cup plain yogurt with 2 tablespoons fresh lemon juice, a pinch of salt, and ¼ teaspoon each of red chili powder, cumin powder, and dried mint. Form the meat mixture into tiny meatballs and bake in a preheated 375ºF oven for 8–10 minutes until completely cooked through. Serve them with the yogurt dipping sauce as an appetizer or a hearty snack.

## Form the Burgers

- You can form the burgers ahead of time and freeze them individually wrapped in plastic.
- Make bite-size burgers to serve as appetizers with a side of chutney.

## Cook the Burgers

- To barbecue these burgers, place them on a hot grill and cook 4–5 minutes on each side until the juices run clear.
- If baking them in an oven, be sure to flip them at least once during the cooking process to ensure even browning of the burgers.

GROUND MEAT

# MINCED CHICKEN WITH SPINACH

Ground chicken and spinach combine to create a simple and highly flavorful dish

Adding spinach to ground chicken is a great way to increase the nutritional value of a high-meat-content dish. In India this dish is traditionally served during the winter, when spinach and other leafy greens fill the markets. Ground chicken does very well in this recipe since it can carry the strong flavor of spinach and blend into it.

I like to serve this with fresh-made warm naan and some raita on the side. You can always swap the ground chicken for lamb or turkey, and the flavor will vary accordingly. During months when fresh spinach is not readily available, you can definitely substitute frozen spinach. *Yield: Serves 3–4*

## Ingredients:

1 teaspoon cumin seeds

2 tablespoons vegetable oil

1 medium onion, finely chopped

1 pound lean ground chicken

1 large tomato, roughly chopped

1/2 teaspoon red chili powder

1/2 teaspoon coriander powder

1/2 teaspoon cumin powder

1/2 teaspoon garam masala powder

6 cups chopped spinach

Salt, to taste

*Minced Chicken with Spinach*

- Sauté cumin seeds in hot oil until they start to sizzle. Add onion and ground chicken and fry until lightly browned.

- Stir in tomatoes and spices and cook until tomatoes soften and begin to pulp.

- Add spinach and salt and simmer covered 15–20 minutes until chicken is completely cooked.

Use frozen chopped spinach instead of fresh to lessen the cooking time. Thoroughly thaw the spinach and squeeze out excess moisture by wringing it in a kitchen towel. You will find frozen chopped spinach and frozen whole leaves in most grocery stores. Avoid the frozen whole spinach; this recipe requires chopped leaves and it would be hard to finely chop a lump of defrosted leaves.

**Chicken Sandwiches:** This recipe's leftovers can be used to make healthy, hearty sandwiches. Simply place a generous helping of the minced chicken between thick slices of buttered bread and grill in a panini press until toasted and crisp. Serve with a tangy chutney and add a large salad to make a quick, balanced lunch.

*Fry the Minced Chicken*

- Be sure to break the chicken up well while frying with the onions.
- You can substitute lean ground turkey for the chicken.

*Prepare the Spinach*

- Always add the spinach toward the end of the cooking process when the chicken is almost cooked.
- To avoid the spinach forming into lumps, mix it well with the ground chicken and spices.

GROUND MEAT

# CHICKEN-STUFFED ZUCCHINI
## Hollowed-out zucchini are topped with sautéed ground chicken

Zucchini have a mild flavor and are therefore a wonderful base for a robustly flavored filling. I was determined to create an Indian-inspired zucchini recipe after I had a delicious Italian version filled with a succulent meat sauce and topped with cheese. Here, ground chicken sautéed with an array of spices and fresh cilantro create a wonderful balance with the zucchini.

Zucchini are high in water content, but hollowing them out will reduce their moisture and prevent them from becoming soggy while they bake. This dish is best eaten warm, so be sure to serve it fresh out of the oven. You can pair these stuffed zucchini with a side of dal and some rice to complete the meal. *Yield: Serves 3–4*

### Ingredients:

1 teaspoon cumin seeds

1 teaspoon coriander seeds

1 teaspoon fennel seeds

2 tablespoons vegetable oil

1 tablespoon minced garlic

1 pound lean ground chicken

$^1/_2$ teaspoon red chili powder

$^1/_2$ teaspoon coriander powder

$^1/_2$ teaspoon cumin powder

$^1/_2$ teaspoon garam masala powder

2 tablespoons tomato paste

Salt, to taste

2 tablespoons minced fresh cilantro

4 zucchini, halved and hollowed

*Chicken-Stuffed Zucchini*

- Sauté cumin, coriander, and fennel seeds in hot oil until they start to sizzle. Add garlic and ground chicken and fry until lightly browned.

- Stir in spice powders and tomato paste and simmer 10–15 minutes until chicken is completely cooked. Add salt and cilantro, then set aside.

- Fill zucchini boats with minced chicken mixture. Bake in a preheated 375°F oven 20–25 minutes until zucchini are tender.

When selecting zucchini for this recipe, choose ones that are of medium size and firm to the touch. These will generally have maximum flavor and not a lot of seeds inside. During the summer months, when the farmers' markets are bursting with fresh produce, you can use ripe yellow zucchini instead of the green.

## MAKE IT EASY

If you plan to serve this dish at a dinner party or make it for a large crowd, save the assembly of the zucchini boats for immediately before baking. You can make the meat filling ahead of time, even a day or two in advance, and store it in the fridge. The meat can also be cooked well in advanced and frozen for up to 3-4 weeks. When you're ready to serve, fill the zucchini and place them in the oven to bake.

*Prepare the Filling*

*Prepare the Zucchini*

- Be sure to cook the meat until all the excess moisture has evaporated. The filling needs to be fairly thick and dry so that the zucchini will not get soggy while baking.

- You can make the filling a day or two ahead of time and store it in the fridge. Let it come to room temperature before stuffing the zucchini.

- Slice off the tops of the zucchini and discard.

- Cut the zucchini lengthwise through the middle. Using a spoon, scoop out the soft flesh and seeds.

- Wipe away any moisture and make sure the insides of the zucchini are completely dry before filling them.

# LAMB & LENTIL STEW

## Tender lamb and hearty lentils are slowly simmered to form a rich, aromatic stew

Stews are great to cook on lazy weekends—they are usually quick to prep and fill the house with a wonderful aroma while they slowly simmer for a couple of hours. Sundays are my pick for a slow-simmering meal, and this stew is a family favorite.

Split-pea lentils are a perfect companion to lamb since they retain their shape after long cooking times and are robust enough to stand up to the strong flavors of lamb. If you don't have a pressure cooker, you can simmer the stew over low heat on the stove top. Cooking times will generally vary depending on the cut of lamb used.

Serve this stew with a crusty bread, or for a more ethnic version, pair it with warm naan. *Yield: Serves 3–4*

## Ingredients:

2 tablespoons vegetable oil

1 teaspoon cumin seeds

1 teaspoon coriander seeds

1 teaspoon fennel seeds

1 medium onion, finely chopped

1 teaspoon minced ginger

1 teaspoon minced garlic

1/4 teaspoon turmeric powder

1/2 teaspoon red chili powder

1 teaspoon coriander powder

1 large tomato, finely chopped

1/2 teaspoon salt

1 1/2 cups yellow split-pea lentils, rinsed

1 pound medium lamb pieces, bone-in

3 cups water

*Lamb and Lentil Stew*

- Heat oil in a pressure cooker and sauté cumin, coriander, and fennel seeds until they start to sizzle. Add onion, ginger, and garlic and fry until onions are lightly browned.

- Stir in spice powders, tomatoes, and salt and cook until tomatoes soften and begin to pulp.

- Mix in lentils, lamb, and water and cook on full pressure for 30–35 minutes until meat is tender.

Depending on the cut of meat used, cooking times will vary drastically. Lamb shoulder is generally used for making Indian curries since the meat become extremely tender after a long simmering and literally falls off the bone. However, shoulder cuts usually contain more bones compared to other cuts, so you may want to use cuts from the leg to get more bang for your buck.

The yellow split-pea lentils used in this recipe take a long time to cook, making them perfect to pair with meat. However, if you have trouble finding them, you can use other lentils, such as the red or brown ones. Keep in mind, though, that these lentils are often quick cooking, and you might want to add them in the middle of the cooking process to prevent them from disintegrating into the stew.

## Wash the Lentils

- Wash the lentils in cool water and a colander before using in the recipe.

- Split-pea lentils have a meatier and more robust flavor than other lentils and can stand up nicely to lamb.

- They also require a much longer cooking time, which makes them perfect for pairing with meat or using in slow-cooked soups and stews.

## Pressure-Cook the Stew

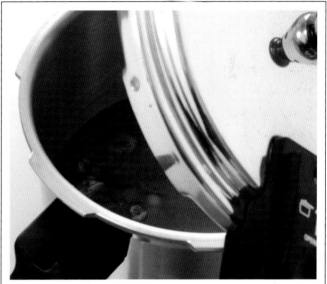

- A pressure cooker will drastically shorten the cooking time of this dish.

- You can also cook it in a normal pot over low heat on the stove top. Cover the pot and let the stew simmer slowly to develop all the flavors.

- Keep in mind that you may need to add extra water and increase the cooking time.

# BLACK PEPPER LAMB

**Boneless chunks of lamb are sautéed with coarse ground pepper and cooked in yogurt**

In southern India, curry leaves and black pepper are commonly used to flavor meat dishes. Freshly ground pepper adds a mild smokiness to the lamb, and the yogurt gives it a slight tang. Curry leaves are readily available at most ethnic stores, but they can be omitted if you find it hard to get your hands on them.

The lamb requires plenty of time to cook, and it is best to let it simmer over low heat. Be sure to check on it at regular intervals to prevent it from getting dry by adding a bit of water as needed. The end result should be extremely tender pieces of lamb coated in a thick gravy. Serve with either roti or rice and a side salad. *Yield: Serves 3–4*

## Ingredients:

2 tablespoons vegetable oil

1 teaspoon cumin seeds

5–6 curry leaves

1 tablespoon minced garlic

1 medium onion, sliced

1 pound cubed lean boneless lamb

1 tablespoon black pepper, freshly ground

$1/2$ cup plain yogurt, beaten

2 cups water

Salt, to taste

*Black Pepper Lamb*

- Heat oil in a deep pan and sauté cumin seeds and curry leaves until they start to sizzle.

- Add garlic and onion and fry until onions are lightly browned.

- Stir in lamb, pepper, yogurt, water, and salt. Cook covered for 45 minutes until lamb is tender.

## Chop the Lamb

- Trim the lamb of any excess fat and cut into bite-size pieces.

- The smaller the pieces of meat, the faster it will cook.

## Simmer the Lamb

- Always cook lamb covered over low heat for best results.

- Remember to stir and check the moisture level at regular intervals to prevent the

meat from sticking to the bottom of the pan.

- Making sure the meat has enough moisture to cook in will prevent it from drying up and burning.

LAMB

# LAMB WITH DRIED APRICOTS

## Tender lamb simmered with dried apricots creates a sweet blend of flavors

Lamb pairs wonderfully with sweet flavors, and slow-cooking it with dried apricots is a great way to do so. Dried apricots are often used in rich meat dishes served during weddings and other special occasions.

I like leaving the apricots whole, but you can chop them into halves or quarters if you prefer them to blend into the curry. Because the meat is cooked for a long time, the apricots literally melt in your mouth. Although this may appear to be a rich and heavy dish, it is simple enough to pull together. I love to serve this at dinner parties to make my guests feel as though I've slaved all day just for them. *Yield: Serves 3–4*

## Ingredients:

1 pound lamb pieces, bone-in

1 cup yogurt, beaten

1 teaspoon cumin powder

1 teaspoon coriander powder

$1/2$ teaspoon red chili powder

1 teaspoon garam masala powder

2 tablespoons vegetable oil

1 medium onion, sliced

1 cinnamon stick

15 dried apricots

$2^1/_2$ cups water

Salt, to taste

*Lamb with Dried Apricots*

- Marinate lamb with yogurt and spices for at least an hour.

- Heat oil in a deep nonstick pan and fry onion and cinnamon stick until onion starts to brown.

- Add marinated lamb, apricots, water, and salt. Cook covered over low heat for about an hour until lamb is tender.

86

Dried apricots can be easily found at most local grocery stores in the baking section, alongside the nuts and raisins. They are generally deep yellow in color and are often sold in small packs. Dried apricots are fairly sweet when cooked and impart a rich flavor to this recipe. You can substitute raisins, but keep in mind that the overall flavor of the dish will differ.

This dish tastes even better the next day, after it has had time to sit and the flavors intensify, so be sure to save some leftovers. It also freezes really well and can stay good for up to 3 weeks. To freeze, let it cool completely to room temperature, and then place it in tightly sealed freezer-friendly containers. It is always a good idea to freeze in smaller batches of 2–3 servings each to enable quick and easy defrosting.

## Marinate the Lamb

- Place the lamb, yogurt, and spices in a large glass bowl and mix well to coat.

- Cover the bowl with plastic wrap and let it sit in the fridge overnight for best results. If pressed for time, marinate the meat for at least an hour before cooking.

## Dried Apricots

- Dried apricots have a distinct sweet flavor, and they will literally melt in your mouth once the dish is done.

- They can be found in most any supermarket.

# MARINATED LAMB CHOPS

Lamb chops marinated in a blend of spices and yogurt are extra tender and juicy

Marinating meat in yogurt is a great way to tenderize it. In this recipe, lamb chops are marinated in a blend of spices and yogurt for a couple of hours to enable the flavors to penetrate into the meat. For best results, marinate the chops overnight in the fridge, and let them come to room temperature before cooking.

You can make a really fancy meal by serving this dish with a saffron pilaf and a mildly spiced raita for dipping. Once the chops are cooked through and ready to serve, let them rest for a few minutes to allow the juices to redistribute. This will ensure that every bite of meat is perfectly tender and juicy. *Yield: Serves 3–4*

## Ingredients:

1 cup yogurt, beaten

1 teaspoon cumin powder

1 teaspoon coriander powder

1/2 teaspoon black pepper

1/2 teaspoon red chili powder

1 teaspoon garam masala powder

1/2 teaspoon salt

2 tablespoons vegetable oil

2 tablespoons fresh lemon juice

8 lamb rib chops, trimmed of extra fat

*Marinated Lamb Chops*

- Combine all the ingredients except the lamb in a large shallow bowl.

- Add the lamb and stir to coat well. Cover and marinate in the refrigerator for at least 3 hours or overnight.

- Place the lamb on a greased baking sheet, discarding any excess marinade. Bake in a preheated 425°F oven 25–20 minutes until meat is tender and cooked through.

88

## Prepare the Chops

- Ask your butcher to "french" the lamb chops, meaning that the meat will be trimmed from the end of the bone to make the chop clean to hold.

- Marinate the chops overnight in the fridge for best results.

## Grill the Chops

- You can use a grill instead of the oven to cook the chops.

- Cook them 4–5 minutes on each side until grill marks form and the lamb is firm to the touch.

LAMB

# SAFFRON LAMB CURRY

## Lamb curry infused with saffron will leave your home wafting in warm aromas

Saffron is undoubtedly one of the most expensive spices available. It therefore goes without saying that when added to any dish, especially a robust lamb curry, saffron infuses it will a wonderful aroma. You may think twice before shelling out the money, but remember that a little saffron goes a long way in infusing its strong, sweet flavor into any dish.

Because this curry is so rich in flavor, you may want to serve it with something like naan or plain white rice to completely enjoy its robustness. If you're planning a meal for a crowd and would like to include more Indian choices, you can also add a dal and side of sautéed vegetables. *Yield: Serves 3–4*

### Ingredients:

2 bay leaves

4–5 whole cloves

4–5 whole cardamoms

1 large onion, finely chopped

2 tablespoons vegetable oil

1/2 teaspoon chili powder

1 teaspoon coriander powder

1 teaspoon cumin powder

1 pound lamb pieces, bone-in

1 cup yogurt, beaten

2 cups water

1 teaspoon saffron threads

Salt, to taste

2 tablespoons minced fresh cilantro

*Saffron Lamb Curry*

- Sauté the whole spices and onion in hot oil until lightly browned.

- Add the spice powders, lamb, and yogurt and cook for a couple of minutes until well mixed.

- Stir in the water, saffron, and salt and cook covered for about an hour until the lamb is tender. Pierce the lamb with a fork to test it; it should literally fall from the bone and break apart.

- Garnish with fresh cilantro and serve.

Saffron is a sweet, fragrant spice derived from the dried stigma of a particular crocus. It imparts a deep, rich color to clear liquids and is often used to add flecks of color to pilafs. Although it may cost a small fortune compared to other kitchen spices, saffron is used in fairly small amounts and can be kept a long time if stored in a cool, dark, dry place.

## GREEN ● LIGHT

The addition of saffron to this dish is what makes it stand out from regular curries. However, if you find it hard to find a good-quality saffron, you can leave it out. The curry will not end up being one of the most exotically flavored you've ever had, but will still be quite nice to enjoy with some plain basmati rice or warm, fresh roti.

### Prepare the Saffron

- Saffron is a very robust spice, and a little goes a long way.

- You can store saffron for a long time in a tight container in a cool, dark place.

### Simmer the Curry

- Let the curry simmer over low heat so that the saffron flavor can permeate through the lamb.

- Adding saffron to this curry gives it a delicate, sweet, aromatic flavor that can't be matched by any other spice.

# LAMB & POTATO STEW

## Classic meat and potatoes come together in this simple, light stew

Meat and potatoes in a curry is fairly common in Indian cuisine. It is said that potatoes can always be found in an Indian kitchen, no matter what the season. I prefer to use bone-in pieces of lamb in a stew like this because the bones infuse an added flavor to the curry. However, if you prefer to use boneless chunks of meat, they will work well, too.

When I'm pressed for time and unable to let this stew slowly simmer on the stove, I use a pressure cooker and the meal is ready in half the time. The only problem with pressure-cooking is that the potatoes may overcook and turn to mush. For best results, old-fashioned slow stove-top cooking is the better way to go. *Yield: Serves 3–4*

## Ingredients:

4–5 whole cloves

4–5 whole cardamoms

1 cinnamon stick

1 teaspoon cumin seeds

1 large onion, finely chopped

2 tablespoons vegetable oil

2 medium tomatoes, finely chopped

1 teaspoon minced ginger

$1/_2$ teaspoon chili powder

1 teaspoon coriander powder

1 teaspoon cumin powder

$1/_2$ teaspoon garam masala powder

1 pound lamb pieces, bone-in

3 cups water

2 medium potatoes

Salt, to taste

*Lamb and Potato Stew*

- Sauté whole spices, cumin seeds, and onion in hot oil until onion is lightly browned.

- Add tomatoes, ginger, and spice powders and cook for a couple of minutes until tomatoes soften and pulp.

- Add lamb and water and cook covered for about 40 minutes.

- Add potatoes and salt and cook covered for another 20 minutes until lamb is tender and potatoes are cooked through.

To cook this dish in a pressure cooker, add enough liquid to completely immerse the meat and potatoes. Let the dish then cook to full pressure, and allow it to simmer for a couple of extra minutes to ensure that the meat is completely cooked through and tender. The one downside to this method of cooking is that the potatoes may get overcooked and break up into the curry. If the potatoes are not too large, you may just want to cut then in halves instead of quarters to prevent them from breaking easily. If cooking on the stove top in a regular pot, it is very important to check at regular intervals to make sure that there is enough liquid to cook the meat and potatoes in. If you notice the moisture start to dry up, add a bit more water and lower the heat. Stir occasionally to prevent the meat from sticking to the bottom of the pan and burning.

## Partially Cook the lamb

- Let the lamb simmer over low heat for about 40–45 minutes before adding the potatoes.

- This will enable the meat to cook partially through and then continue to cook with the potatoes. That way, the meat and potatoes will become tender at about the same time and the potatoes won't overcook.

## Prepare the Potatoes

- Try to use similar-size potatoes so that they can be quartered evenly. Peel and cut them into quarters.

- Pierce potatoes with a fork to check for doneness. They should be soft through the middle, yet still hold their shape in the curry.

- Turn off the heat before the potatoes break apart. If the meat needs more time to tenderize and the potatoes have already cooked through, remove the potatoes and set them aside. Once the meat has completely cooked, add potatoes back into the curry and serve.

LAMB

93

# MUSTARD FISH CURRY
## Mustard seeds add a distinct flavor to a simple fish curry

This is a mildly spiced yet highly flavorful fish curry that can be done in no time. The mustard and nigella seeds combine to add a robust aromatic flavor. Although I've used tilapia in this recipe, you can include any firm whitefish, including cod, halibut, or haddock. When picking a fish for this dish, opt for one that has a subtle and mild flavor to prevent it from overpowering the overall taste of the curry.

Serve this curry with a side of plain basmati rice. For best results, I suggest using deep bowls and topping the rice with a generous helping of the curry—almost enough to drown the rice in. *Yield: Serves 3–4*

## Ingredients:

2 teaspoons mustard seeds

1 teaspoon nigella seeds

1 teaspoon minced ginger

1 medium onion, finely chopped

2 tablespoons vegetable oil

1/4 teaspoon turmeric powder

1/2 teaspoon red chili powder

1 teaspoon coriander powder

1 large tomato, finely chopped

1 cup water

3 tilapia/halibut fillets, cut into medium pieces

Salt, to taste

*Mustard Fish Curry*

- Sauté mustard and nigella seeds, ginger, and onions in hot oil until onions are lightly browned.

- Add the spice powders and tomatoes and cook for a couple of minutes until tomatoes soften and pulp.

- Add water, fish pieces, and salt and cook covered 10–15 minutes until fish is done.

**Mustard Shrimp Curry:** You can vary this recipe by using frozen shrimp. Peel and devein 12–15 large shrimp and add them to the curry instead of the fish. Let the curry simmer for a couple of minutes until the shrimp turns pink and starts to firm. Serve over a bowl of plain basmati rice.

This curry would work really well with any firm whitefish like halibut, haddock, cod, and even trout. Be sure to cut the pieces large enough so that they do not break and disintegrate into the curry. Avoid using a strong-flavored fish like salmon, since it would overpower the dish and detract from the delicate flavors of the curry.

*Prepare the Fish*

- You can use any firm white-fish for this recipe, including haddock, cod, or halibut.
- It is best to use fish fillets to avoid any bones that can fall into and mix with the curry.

*Sauté the Onions*

- Cook the onions until they become soft and start to brown along the edges.
- They will continue to cook after adding the spices and tomatoes, so make sure not to brown them too much in the beginning.

95

FISH & SHRIMP

# HOT & SOUR FISH STEW

## Hot and sour flavors combine to give this stew a burst of flavor

Hot and sour is a wonderful flavor combination for a rich, hearty stew like this. The heat from the chilies and tartness of the tamarind will linger on your palate for a long time. I like to make a large pot of this stew during the winter months and serve it over a bowl full of rice.

Tilapia is fairly mild in flavor and takes on the intense flavors of this dish really well. You can alter the recipe by using either halibut or red snapper instead of tilapia. I would, however, steer away from using a much stronger-tasting fish like salmon, since the robust flavor will interfere with the richness of the stew. *Yield: Serves 3–4*

## Ingredients:

1 teaspoon cumin seeds

1 teaspoon mustard seeds

1 teaspoon minced garlic

1 medium onion, finely chopped

2 tablespoons vegetable oil

1/4 teaspoon turmeric powder

1/2 teaspoon red chili powder

1 teaspoon coriander powder

1 large tomato, finely chopped

1 teaspoon minced green chilies

1 tablespoon tomato paste

1 teaspoon tamarind concentrate

2 cups water

3 tilapia fillets, cut into medium pieces

Salt, to taste

*Hot and Sour Fish Stew*

- Sauté cumin and mustard seeds, garlic, and onions in hot oil until onions are lightly browned.

- Add spice powders, tomatoes, green chilies, tomato paste, and tamarind and cook for a couple of minutes until tomatoes soften and pulp.

- Add water, fish pieces, and salt and cook covered 10–15 minutes until fish is done.

You can make this a hearty seafood stew by adding 2 or 3 different kinds of fish and seafood. If you plan on adding shrimp to the recipe, peel and devein them before cooking. A variety of fish like salmon, trout, and halibut would work extremely well in this dish.

This stew tastes even better the next day, after all the flavors have had more time to infuse and blend, so you'll definitely want to save some leftovers. You can make an extra batch and freeze it for a busy weeknight. Let the stew cool completely to room temperature, then store it in an airtight freezer-friendly container. The day before you plan to serve, defrost the stew in the fridge overnight, then simply bring the stew to a full boil before serving.

## Tamarind Concentrate

- Tamarind concentrate is sold in tiny containers and can be stored in the fridge for ages.

- The flavor is rather tart and robust, so reduce the amount if you like your food less tangy.

## Simmer the Stew

- Let the stew simmer to merge all the flavors.

- This stew is best enjoyed piping hot on cold winter nights with a side of warm rustic bread.

- Leftovers taste even better the next day, after the flavors have had time to blend in.

FISH & SHRIMP

# CHILI SHRIMP
## A quick, spicy stir-fried shrimp delight

Shrimp is one of my favorite quick-fix seafood picks for any evening I'm in a rush. I always make sure I have a bag of store-bought uncooked and peeled shrimp in my freezer. On days when I need to whip up something quick, simple, and delicious, all I do is thaw a few frozen shrimp in a big bowl of water, and within minutes I'm all set to serve a hearty dinner.

I love this recipe for its quick, spicy, and simple characteristics. It is a breeze to make and is a definite crowd pleaser. As with most recipes, you can always cut down on the spice level by decreasing the amount of chili powder, or omitting it altogether if you can't take the heat. *Yield: Serves 3–4*

## Ingredients:

1 teaspoon minced garlic

1 medium onion, sliced

2 tablespoons vegetable oil

15–20 large shrimp, peeled and deveined

$1/4$ teaspoon turmeric powder

$1/2$ teaspoon red chili powder

1 teaspoon coriander powder

1 tablespoon tomato paste

Salt, to taste

2 tablespoons fresh lemon juice

*Chili Shrimp*

- Sauté garlic and onions in hot oil until the onions are lightly browned.

- Add shrimp, spices, tomato paste, and salt and stir-fry 4–6 minutes until shrimp turns pink and is cooked through.

- Sprinkle with lemon juice and serve with warm plain rice.

A bag of shrimp in the freezer can come in handy when you are pressed for time and need something that will cook fast. For best results, buy large, uncooked, peeled shrimp. They freeze wonderfully and literally take minutes to thaw. Simply place them in a large bowl of cold water and let them sit for a few minutes until the shrimp come to room temperature.

## • • • • RECIPE VARIATION • • • •

**Stir-Fried Shrimp with Veggies:** Sauté 1 teaspoon each of minced garlic and ginger in 1 tablespoon of oil. Add 1 medium sliced onion, 12–15 large peeled shrimp, and ¼ teaspoon each of red chili powder, cumin powder, and coriander powder. Fry until shrimp turn opaque. Add ½ cup each of sliced green pepper, carrots, and red peppers and stir-fry with 2 tablespoons of tomato paste until well coated. Season and serve.

*Prepare the Shrimp*

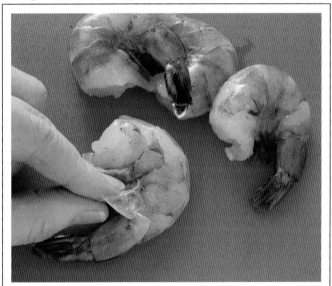

- When using frozen shrimp, thaw them in a bowlful of cold water for a couple of minutes. Then rinse and pat dry.
- You can leave the tails on the shrimp for a nice presentation.

*Stir-Fry the Shrimp*

- Be sure to stir-fry the shrimp thoroughly so that they get completely coated with the spices.
- For best results, use a large nonstick wok to enable the ingredients to mix well.

FISH & SHRIMP

# COCONUT FISH CURRY

## A mild, flavorful curry made with coconut milk and spices

This curry comes from the southern part of India that is abundantly rich in both coconuts and seafood. The spices used are fairly mild to allow the sweet flavors of the coconut milk to shine through. Although traditionally fresh coconut milk is used, you can always substitute readily available store-bought canned coconut milk.

This curry is great with a helping of plain white rice, and can even be thinned downed a little to be enjoyed as a hearty soup. You can use any kind of fish in the recipe, such as tilapia, trout, or halibut, or even shrimp, and each variation will impart its own delicious blend of flavor. To bump up the heat level of this recipe, add chopped fresh green chilies along with coconut milk. *Yield: Serves 3–4*

KNACK INDIAN COOKING

**Ingredients:**

4–5 fresh curry leaves

2 garlic cloves, minced

2 tablespoons vegetable oil

1 medium onion, sliced

1 teaspoon coriander powder

1/4 teaspoon turmeric powder

1/2 teaspoon red chili powder

1 medium tomato, finely chopped

1 1/4 cups coconut milk

3 salmon fillets, cut into medium pieces

1 teaspoon dried fenugreek leaves

Salt, to taste

*Coconut Fish Curry*

- Sauté curry leaves, garlic, and onions in hot oil until the onions are lightly browned.

- Add the spice powders and tomatoes and cook for a few minutes until tomatoes soften and pulp.

- Add coconut milk, fish, fenugreek leaves, and salt and cook covered 10–15 minutes until fish is done.

Canned coconut milk is readily available at most grocery stores, usually in the baking or international foods aisle. Always shake the can well before using, since coconut milk tends to separate, leaving a thick creamy layer on top and the clear liquid at the bottom. These days many stores also carry a light version of coconut milk, which has less fat content and would work equally well as a substitute for the regular milk in any recipe.

**Coconut Chicken Curry:** You can easily alter this recipe by substituting chicken. Cut the boneless chicken into bite-size pieces and add it to the curry at the same time the fish would have been added. Keep in mind that chicken takes slightly longer to cook, so you will need to let the curry simmer for a while longer, about 20–25 minutes.

*Canned Coconut Milk*

- When using canned coconut milk, be sure to shake the can well first since the cream tends to separate and remain on top.
- For a low-fat version, use light coconut milk.

*Simmer the Curry*

- Let the curry simmer over a low heat to allow the flavor of the coconut milk to permeate the fish.
- After the curry comes to a full boil, you should turn the heat down to a simmer.

FISH & SHRIMP

# MASALA BAKED FISH
A blend of spices add a delicate burst of flavor to oven-baked fish

I have always loved grilled fish and can never resist the strong temptation to sneak in as much flavors as I can before placing it in the oven. Here I've used a simple blend of chili, turmeric, and coriander to spice up fresh fillets of salmon. The delicate spice blend works perfectly with the strong flavor of salmon and makes it a treat for the palate.

On warm summer afternoons, I love to throw the fish on a warm grill and cook it until the ends slightly char to a rich, deep color. Then I place the perfectly grilled fish on a platter of fresh, crisp lettuce and thinly sliced onions. Sprinkle some fresh lemon juice on top, and serve with warm, crusty bread. *Yield: Serves 3–4*

### Ingredients:

2 salmon fillets, halved lengthwise

$1/2$ teaspoon red chili powder

$1/4$ teaspoon turmeric powder

1 teaspoon coriander powder

$1/2$ teaspoon salt

Pinch black pepper

2 tablespoons lemon juice

*Masala Baked Fish*

- Rub fish with spices, salt, pepper, and lemon juice on both sides to coat well.

- Wrap tightly in aluminum foil and bake in a preheated 375ºF oven 20–25 minutes until fish is done.

**Masala Fish Sandwich:** Make a dip by whisking 1 cup plain yogurt; ¼ teaspoon each of red chili powder, cumin powder, and dried mint; and a pinch of salt in a bowl to blend well. Lightly toast 2 thick slices of bread and place fresh lettuce, slices of tomatoes, and red bell peppers on a slice. Top with baked fish, sprinkle on the yogurt, and sandwich with another slice of toast.

**Grilled Fish Salad:** In a large bowl, combine ½ cup olive oil, 2 tablespoons fresh lemon juice, ¼ teaspoon cumin powder, and a pinch of salt. Whisk to blend well. Add 3 cups fresh baby spinach, ½ cup thinly sliced onions, and 1 cup thinly sliced cucumbers to the bowl. Roughly chop the baked fish, place it in bowl, and lightly fold the vegetables and fish into dressing to coat well.

*Prepare the Fish*

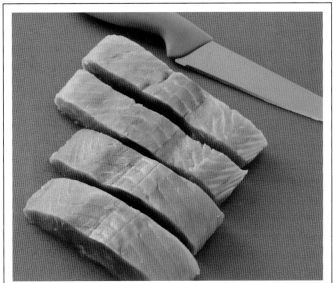

*Season the Fish*

- For best results, use fish that is as fresh as possible. If using frozen fish, allow it to thaw in the fridge for a couple of hours before bringing it to room temperature.

- You can use any firm fish in place of salmon, like haddock or halibut, for this recipe.

- Slice the fish lengthwise and season well with the spices.

- Be sure not to let the fish sit too long in the marinade, as the lemon juice will start to cook it.

FISH & SHRIMP

# TAMARIND SHRIMP
## Shrimp sautéed in a spicy, tart tamarind sauce

Tamarind Shrimp is one of my personal favorite recipes to make when I'm alone at home and need something to perk me up. The spicy, tart flavors of this dish will awaken your senses and take you to a whole new world. It is important to use good-quality tamarind concentrate for this recipe, devoid of any salt or additives.

Since shrimp tends not to have a strong flavor, it is a perfect candidate to pair with the robustness of tamarind. Tamarind can be overpowering, but the tomatoes add a bit of sweetness to help smooth out the strong taste. I love to serve this over a bowl of plain white rice, with some chilled lemonade to complement the tanginess. *Yield: Serves 3–4*

## Ingredients:

1 teaspoon mustard seeds

2 garlic cloves, minced

1 medium onion, sliced

2 tablespoons vegetable oil

$^1/_2$ teaspoon red chili powder

$^1/_2$ teaspoon coriander powder

1 medium tomato, finely chopped

1 tablespoon tomato paste

1 teaspoon tamarind concentrate

15–20 large shrimp, peeled and deveined

Salt, to taste

*Tamarind Shrimp*

- Sauté mustard seeds, garlic, and onions in hot oil until the onions are lightly browned.

- Add chili and coriander powders, tomatoes, tomato paste, and tamarind. Cook for a few minutes until tomatoes soften and pulp.

- Add shrimp and salt and stir-fry until shrimp are done, about 8–10 minutes.

Tamarind concentrate can be found at most ethnic grocery stores. It is often sold in small plastic containers and can keep for a long time when stored in the fridge. Tamarind concentrate dissolves well in water and can be easily thinned down. Since the flavor of the pure concentrate is quite tart and robust, a little goes a long way.

## GREEN ● LIGHT

I often like making an extra batch of this dish to save for a later date. Let it cool to room temperature before you store it in a tight plastic container and freeze it. The shrimp freezes really well, and the flavors get even more concentrated as time goes by. Before you are ready to serve, let it thaw overnight in the fridge before heating it in the microwave.

### Fry the Tomatoes

### Add the Shrimp

- Always use fresh, ripe, plump tomatoes, as they will have a robust flavor.

- Canned tomatoes often add a rich sweetness, so you will want to avoid using them in curries.

- Cook the tomatoes well, breaking them up with the back of your ladle to help pulp them nicely.

- You can add a tablespoon or two of water if they start to dry up.

- The shrimp will hardly take any time to cook.

- Remember to mix the shrimp well with the sauce, and take them off the heat once they turn opaque and begin to firm up.

# POTATOES WITH PEAS & CUMIN

Lightly spiced potatoes sautéed with whole cumin seeds and green peas

Jeera Alu, potatoes sautéed with whole cumin seeds, is a widely popular home-cooked Indian side dish. Since potatoes are one of the most commonly used vegetables in Indian cuisine, there are many simple home recipes that feature them as the main ingredient.

In this recipe, whole cumin seeds are sautéed in hot oil for a few seconds to toast them and bring out the fragrance before adding them to the potatoes and other spices. This allows the cumin seeds to release their aromatic flavor into the oil, which in turn coats the potatoes and imparts a delicate taste. The frozen peas add a slight sweetness and texture to this fairly quick and simple dish. *Yield: Serves 3–4*

## Ingredients:

- 1 tablespoon cumin seeds
- 2 tablespoons vegetable oil
- 3 medium potatoes, cubed
- 1/2 teaspoon red chili powder
- 1/4 teaspoon turmeric powder
- 1/4 teaspoon amchoor powder
- 1 cup frozen peas, thawed
- Salt, to taste

*Potatoes with Peas and Cumin*

- Sauté cumin seeds in hot oil until they start to sizzle.

- Add potatoes and spice powders and fry 15–20 minutes, stirring occasionally, until potatoes are tender.

- Add peas and salt and stir-fry for a few more minutes to mix well.

## ···· RECIPE VARIATION ····

**Sautéed Cauliflower with Cumin:** Cut a medium cauliflower into bite-size florets and place them in a bowl of cold water for 15–20 minutes. Follow the recipe as directed, swapping the potatoes for the cauliflower and omitting the peas. Keep in mind that the cauliflower will take about half the time to cook as the potatoes.

*Prepare the Potatoes*

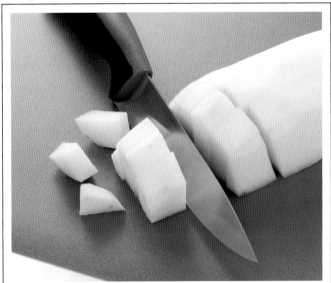

*Fry Cumin Seeds*

- Cut the potatoes into bite-size pieces to lessen the cooking time.

- You can soak the chopped potatoes in a bowlful of cold water for a couple of minutes to get rid of excess starch.

- Always make sure that the oil is not smoking hot before adding cumin seeds; otherwise, they will darken and pop immediately.

- Cumin seeds burn quickly, so add the potatoes to the pan as soon as they start to sizzle, usually after a few seconds.

# MASHED SWEET POTATOES
## A healthier alternative to the classic mashed potatoes

This recipe is a perfect blend of East and West. It combines the classic mashed potatoes of the Western world and the more traditional flavors of classic Indian cooking. Sweet potatoes are rich in vitamins and are extremely nutritious. Here I've paired them with a blend of delicate spices to give them a new spin. This adds a slightly spicy and sour flavor that combines perfectly with the sweetness of the potatoes.

I love to serve this as a side with spicy grilled chicken and some roasted vegetables. The sweet potatoes also go well with a side of dal and some warm roti. This dish is best served warm and can easily be made ahead and heated in the microwave right before it is time to eat. *Yield: Serves 3–4*

### Ingredients:

2 large sweet potatoes

$1/2$ teaspoon cumin powder

$1/2$ teaspoon red chili powder

$1/2$ teaspoon coriander powder

$1/2$ teaspoon amchoor powder

Salt, to taste

*Mashed Sweet Potatoes*

- Boil the sweet potatoes in a large pot of water until soft and tender for about 20–25 minutes, then peel and mash them in a bowl with a fork or potato masher.

- Thoroughly mix the spices and salt together in a small bowl. Immediately before serving, sprinkle the spices over the mashed sweet potatoes and fold well to combine.

*Boil the Sweet Potatoes*

- Fill a large pot with water and submerge the sweet potatoes, after making sure to thoroughly scrub them clean. Boil until tender for 20–25 minutes.

- To test for doneness, prick the sweet potatoes with a fork. If it goes in easily, the potatoes are done.

*Mash the Sweet Potatoes*

- Mash the sweet potatoes with a potato masher or a fork while they are still warm.

- This will not only make it easier to pulp them, but will also help infuse the flavors of the spices when they are added.

# EGGPLANT WITH YOGURT

## Sautéed eggplant simmered in a light yogurt sauce

Eggplant is one of the most versatile vegetables and can be made to take on pretty much any kind of flavors. In this recipe, tender slices of eggplant are lightly sautéed and spiced, and then cooked in a bit of yogurt. The yogurt adds a slight tang that enhances the spices. The spices used in this recipe are fairly simple, but combined with the yogurt, add a delicate touch of flavor to the entire dish.

This dish is best enjoyed with a side of freshly made warm roti and a light chutney. You can also serve it alongside a flavorful pilaf with a light chicken dish and some salad. *Yield: Serves 3–4*

**Ingredients:**

1 teaspoon cumin seeds

4 Japanese eggplants, cut into 1-inch pieces

2 tablespoons vegetable oil

1 teaspoon coriander powder

$^1/_2$ teaspoon red chili powder

$^1/_2$ teaspoon turmeric powder

$^1/_2$ teaspoon garam masala powder

$^1/_2$ cup plain yogurt, beaten

Salt, to taste

2 tablespoons minced fresh cilantro

*Eggplant with Yogurt*

- Fry cumin seeds and eggplant in hot oil until eggplant starts to brown and becomes tender.

- Stir the spice powders and yogurt into the eggplant.

- Cook for a couple of minutes until the ingredients are well mixed.

- Season with salt and garnish with fresh cilantro.

### Chop and Soak the Eggplants

- Once you have chopped the eggplants, soak them a large bowl of cold water for a couple of minutes to get rid of the bitterness.

- Soaking them in water will also slow down the dis-

coloration of the chopped eggplants while you prep the rest of the ingredients.

- Make sure to drain and dry the eggplant before adding it to the hot oil.

### Add the Yogurt

- When adding yogurt to a hot pan, beat the yogurt until smooth to prevent it from breaking up and disintegrating as it reaches a hot temperature.

- As you pour in the yogurt, slowly fold the eggplant pieces into it to blend well.

# RUSTIC POTATO CURRY
## A traditional potato curry cooked in a rich tomato base

This traditional potato curry, or Alu Bhaji as it is commonly referred to in India, is often served on the brunch menu along with a deep-fried Indian bread called puri. The potatoes are first boiled until tender and then added to a rich curry made by sautéing onions and tomatoes in a blend of spices.

Any leftovers of this dish can be stored in the fridge for use a day or two later. The leftovers actually tend to taste much better the next day, since as with most curries, the flavors have had enough time to blend in and penetrate through the dish. I love to whip this up on a weeknight and serve it with some rice and a side salad for a quick, healthy dinner.
*Yield: Serves 3–4*

**Ingredients:**

1 teaspoon cumin seeds

1 medium onion, finely chopped

2 tablespoons vegetable oil

$1/4$ teaspoon turmeric powder

$1/2$ teaspoon red chili powder

$1/2$ teaspoon coriander powder

1 medium tomato, finely chopped

3 medium potatoes, boiled and broken into pieces

1 cup water

Salt, to taste

*Rustic Potato Curry*

- Fry cumin seeds and onions in hot oil until onions start to brown and become tender.

- Add the spice powders and tomatoes and cook for a couple of minutes until tomatoes pulp.

- Add potatoes, water, and salt and cook covered another 10–12 minutes.

## · · · · RECIPE VARIATION · · · ·

**Cauliflower and Carrot Curry:** Cut a medium cauliflower into bite-size florets and place them in a bowl of cold water for 15–20 minutes. Peel and chop 2 or 3 carrots into bite-size pieces and set aside. Follow the recipe as directed, swapping the potatoes for the cauliflower and carrots. Let the curry simmer over low heat for 15–20 minutes until the cauliflower and carrots are tender.

*Boil the Potatoes*

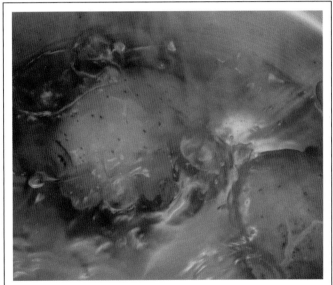

*Break the Potatoes*

- For quick cooking, you can use a microwave to soften the potatoes instead of boiling them on the stove top.

- To microwave, place the potatoes in a large glass bowl filled with water and heat on high 6–8 minutes

until the potatoes are soft and tender.

- Once boiled, either on the stove top or in the microwave, immediately immerse the potatoes in a bowl of cold water to peel the skins off easily.

- Because this is a rustic curry, you will want to avoid the sense of perfection by breaking the potatoes with your fingers instead of chopping them into even sizes.

- Breaking them by hand will give you different shapes and sizes and will add to the overall texture of this curry.

113

# SAUTÉED CABBAGE & CARROTS

## Lightly spiced shredded cabbage and carrots sautéed with mustard seeds

I remember having a dish quite similar to this one a couple of years ago at a friend's place for dinner. Although I've never been a big fan of cabbage cooked the Indian way, this dish somehow stood out and piqued my interest. The spices were subtle, yet added a nice touch to the bland cabbage and carrots. The mustard and cumin seeds were first sautéed in the hot oil, giving them a nice crunch. I love to use any leftovers of this dish as a filling for wraps or sandwiches the next day for lunch. You can serve this as a side dish with some dal and a flavorful spiced pilaf. It also pairs well with a light chicken curry and warm roti or naan. Add a bowl of raita to complete the meal. *Yield: Serves 3–4*

### Ingredients:

1 teaspoon cumin seeds

1 teaspoon mustard seeds

2 tablespoons vegetable oil

2 cups shredded cabbage

1 cup shredded carrots

¼ teaspoon turmeric powder

½ teaspoon red chili powder

½ teaspoon coriander powder

¼ garam masala powder

Salt, to taste

*Sautéed Cabbage and Carrots*

- Sauté the cumin and mustard seeds in hot oil until they start to sizzle.

- Add the cabbage, carrots, spice powders, and salt. Stir-fry for a couple of minutes until the vegetables are cooked and well blended with the spices.

114

## MAKE IT EASY

If you're pressed for time and can't spare a couple of extra minutes to shred the cabbage and carrots, you can use store-bought ready-made coleslaw mix to quicken the preparation time. I usually keep a bag of coleslaw mix in my fridge for days when I need a quick dinner fix. This enables me to cut down on my overall cooking time and get dinner on the table in a flash.

## • • • • RECIPE VARIATION • • • •

**Sautéed Cabbage and Chicken Wraps:** Follow the recipe as directed but add 1 cup shredded cooked chicken breast along with the cabbage and carrots. Warm some flour tortillas in a frying pan, then place about 2–3 tablespoons of the sautéed cabbage and chicken mixture in the middle and fold before rolling tightly to form wraps.

*Shred the Cabbage*

- Slicing the vegetables into thin shreds with a knife can be a daunting task. To make things easier and save time, use a box grater or mandolin to shred the veggies as finely as possible.

- If you're in a time crunch, pick up some ready-made coleslaw mix at the grocery store. It will help you whip up this dish in no time.

*Sauté the Veggies*

- Lightly sauté the cabbage and carrots, making sure not to overcook them.

- You want the veggies to have a slight crunch to add body and texture to the dish.

115

# MUSHROOM CURRY
## A rich mushroom curry simmered in yogurt and a blend of spices

Mushrooms are a great alternative to meat for many vegetarians since they have a strong, meaty texture and can take on heavy flavors. This curry is a wonderful way to treat your guest who may not be able to enjoy a robust chicken curry. The mushrooms are allowed to slowly simmer in a rich blend of spices and yogurt, giving them a rich texture and tremendous flavor.

I love to serve this dish at dinner parties along with some grilled chicken, a dal, pilaf, some naan, and a delicately flavored raita. To make a simple complete meal, serve with some warm, freshly made roti and a salad. Any leftovers can be stored in the fridge or frozen for later use. *Yield: Serves 3–4*

### Ingredients:

1 teaspoon nigella seeds

1 medium onion, finely chopped

2 tablespoons vegetable oil

15 baby button mushrooms, sliced

¹/₄ cup plain yogurt, beaten

1 teaspoon coriander powder

¹/₄ teaspoon turmeric powder

¹/₂ teaspoon red chili powder

¹/₂ teaspoon garam masala powder

¹/₂ cup water

Salt, to taste

*Mushroom Curry*

- Fry nigella seeds and onions in hot oil until onions become tender.

- Add mushrooms and fry for a couple of minutes until all the moisture evaporates and they start to brown.

- Slowly stir in beaten yogurt and add spice powders, water, and salt and cook covered another 10–15 minutes.

## GREEN ● LIGHT

You can use almost any kind of mushroom for this recipe, and white button, shiitake, and portobello mushrooms work extremely well. When preparing mushrooms for cooking, avoid rinsing them in water, as this tends to make them soggy and ruin the texture. Use a damp paper towel or clean cloth to wipe the mushrooms clean without washing them entirely in water. Discard the stems if they seem to be hard and differ in texture from the tops.

## • • • • RECIPE VARIATION • • • •

**Paneer Curry:** You can change this recipe by using fresh paneer instead of mushrooms. Cut about a 250-gram block of paneer into bite-size cubes. Follow the recipe as directed, swapping the mushrooms for the paneer. Be careful while adding the pieces of paneer, as they tend to sputter when they hit hot oil. Garnish with finely chopped fresh cilantro and serve with a side of roti or naan.

*Slice the Mushrooms*

- Wipe the mushroom caps clean with a damp paper towel or clean cloth.

- Discard the stems if they appear to be too tough, and thinly slice the mushrooms.

*Simmer the Curry*

- Slowly stir in the yogurt and blend it well with all the spices and mushrooms, before adding in water.

- Simmer the curry over low heat for 10–15 minutes to allow the flavors to blend in and permeate through the dish.

# SAUTÉED OKRA & ONIONS
## Crisp, fresh okra lightly fried with onions and spices

A quick, simple sauté of fresh okra with sliced onions in a blend of spices is a common everyday dish in most Indian homes. I like to make my version with a slight tang, and the amchoor powder does just that. The okra is stir-fried continuously so that it gets well coated with all the spices and onions.

This dish can come together in a pretty short amount of time and is perfect for busy weeknights. I love to serve it with a quick dal and some rice or roti on the side. Although fresh, crisp okra works best and gives the maximum flavor, you can also opt for frozen chopped okra to save on the prep time. *Yield: Serves 3–4*

**Ingredients:**

1 teaspoon cumin seeds

1 medium onion, finely chopped

3 cups chopped okra

2 tablespoons vegetable oil

$1/4$ teaspoon turmeric powder

$1/2$ teaspoon red chili powder

$1/2$ teaspoon coriander powder

$1/2$ teaspoon amchoor powder

Salt, to taste

*Sautéed Okra and Onions*

- Fry cumin seeds, onions, and okra in hot oil until the okra starts to brown and the stickiness disappears.

- Add the spice powders and salt and stir-fry for a couple minutes until well mixed and the okra is tender and cooked through.

When cooking with fresh okra, try to keep it away from as much moisture as possible, since moisture extracts more stickiness from it. Use a damp cloth to wipe the okra clean, and make sure your knife is wiped dry while chopping it into pieces. When the okra is added to the pan for frying, be sure to stir constantly to prevent it from sticking to the bottom. Constant stirring will also ensure that the spices are well blended with the okra.

#### · · · · RECIPE VARIATION · · · ·

**Sautéed Green Beans with Onions:** Cut green beans into 1-inch pieces after slicing off their ends. Stir-fry the beans with sliced onions in hot oil for 4–6 minutes until they are partially cooked through. Add the spices and stir-fry for another 5–6 minutes until the green beans are completely tender and well coated with the spices.

*Chop the Okra*

- Wipe the okra with a clean, damp cloth to remove any dirt.

- Using a sharp, dry knife, slice off the ends of each okra and chop them into ½-inch pieces.

*Stir-Fry the Okra*

- The okra needs to be stir-fried continuously to prevent its glue from sticking to the pan.

- Once the spices have been added, be sure to continue constantly stirring the okra to allow the spices to blend in evenly.

# CREAMY SPINACH

## A rich, creamy blend of pureed spinach and yogurt

This dish is a simple, quick variation of the classic restaurant favorite Palak Paneer, minus the paneer. Using frozen spinach makes this a breeze to prepare, and the dish comes together easily in no time. Creamy spinach pairs beautifully with a side of warm, freshly made naan and can also be served alongside some plain basmati rice.

I always make sure I have a package or two of frozen spinach in my freezer. It is one of my must-have staples and helps to make dinnertime both quick and nutritious. Sometimes, when I'm pressed for time and rushing to get dinner on the table as fast as possible, I like to make a thinned-down version of this recipe by adding a bit of water or vegetable stock and serve it as a rich soup with warm, crusty bread. *Yield: Serves 3–4*

### Ingredients:

3 garlic cloves, minced

1 tablespoon vegetable oil

1 cup frozen spinach, thawed and pureed

1/2 teaspoon red chili powder

1/2 teaspoon coriander powder

1/2 teaspoon cumin powder

1/2 cup plain yogurt, beaten

Salt, to taste

*Creamy Spinach*

- Sauté garlic in hot oil until fragrant.

- Add pureed spinach, spices, yogurt, and salt. Cook covered 10–15 minutes until blended, stirring occasionally to mix well.

∙∙∙∙ **RECIPE VARIATION** ∙∙∙∙

**Spinach Chicken Curry:** Follow the recipe as directed. Once the spinach starts to come to a boil, add 2 chicken breasts cut into bite-size pieces and about 1 cup water. Mix well and cook covered 8–10 minutes until the chicken is cooked through. Once the chicken is thoroughly cooked, remove from the heat and serve it with fresh-made naan and a side salad.

*Frozen Spinach*

- Follow the package instructions to quickly defrost the spinach.

- Place the thawed spinach in a blender with a bit of water, and puree until smooth.

*Stir Well*

- Stir the pureed spinach and beaten yogurt to blend well.

- Once the mixture heats through, it will start to bubble and spurt out of the pan, so be careful and keep the heat on low to prevent any accidents.

# MASALA GREEN BEANS
## Fresh green beans are lightly sautéed with a blend of spices

I often make this recipe when I need an extra side dish to complement my dinner menu. Fresh-cut green beans are lightly sautéed with a blend of simple everyday spices, and pair well with almost anything. My favorite is to serve this with a rich chicken curry and some naan, but you can also serve it with dal and rice for a quick weeknight dinner.

You can fill warm flour tortillas with the green beans and some fresh lettuce and tomatoes to make a quick and simple wrap for lunch. This dish keeps perfectly well when stored properly in the fridge, and any leftovers can be enjoyed over the next day or two. *Yield: Serves 3–4*

## Ingredients:

1 teaspoon cumin seeds

1 medium onion, sliced

2 tablespoons vegetable oil

1/4 teaspoon turmeric powder

1/2 teaspoon red chili powder

1/2 teaspoon coriander powder

1/2 teaspoon garam masala powder

2 cups chopped green beans

Salt, to taste

1 tablespoon fresh lemon juice

*Masala Green Beans*

- Fry cumin seeds and onions in hot oil until onions start to brown and become tender.

- Add spice powders, green beans, and salt and simmer for a couple minutes until beans are cooked through.

- Sprinkle with lemon juice before serving.

## ·····   RECIPE VARIATION  ····

**Added Veggies:** You can add more vegetables to accompany the green beans. If you decide to add potatoes, chop them into small, bite-size pieces and fry them for 5–6 minutes before adding the beans. Frozen peas should be added in the last 3–4 minutes of the cooking process, whereas chopped fresh carrots can be added at the same time as the beans.

*Chop the Green Beans*

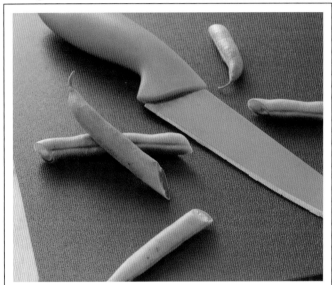

*Squeeze in Lemon Juice*

- Wash and drain the green beans completely and slice off both ends.

- Chop the beans into 1-inch pieces and place them in a bowl of cold water until you

are ready to add them to the pan, to keep them fresh and crisp.

- Make sure to completely drain the beans before adding into the hot pan.

- Squeeze in the fresh lemon juice once the green beans have completely cooked through.

- Lemon juice gives the beans a fresh flavor and adds a slight tang to the entire dish.

# CAULIFLOWER WITH PEAS

## A classic dish of tender cauliflower cooked with green peas

Gobi Matar, cauliflower cooked with peas, is a classic favorite in most Indian kitchens. Since a simple, everyday Indian dinner usually consists of a dal, a vegetable side, and some rice and roti, it is quite common to find quick and simple vegetarian dishes like this one prepared at supper time. Cauliflower is a fairly quick-cooking vegetable, and paired with frozen peas, makes a delightful dish to whip up on busy weeknights.

You can also add a cup of chopped fresh carrots along with the cauliflower to bump up this recipe's nutritional value. Serve it alongside some dal and rice, or pair it with a rich lamb curry and naan for a more exotic treat. *Yield: Serves 3–4*

### Ingredients:

1 teaspoon cumin seeds

3 cups cauliflower florets

$1/4$ teaspoon turmeric powder

$1/2$ teaspoon red chili powder

$1/2$ teaspoon garam masala powder

$1/2$ teaspoon amchoor powder

2 tablespoons vegetable oil

1 cup frozen peas, thawed

Salt, to taste

*Cauliflower with Peas*

- Fry cumin seeds, cauliflower, and spice powders in hot oil until cauliflower starts to become tender, about 8–10 minutes.

- Add peas and salt and cook for a couple minutes to mix well.

···· **RECIPE VARIATION** ····

**Cauliflower with Potatoes:** To make the classic restaurant favorite Alu Gobi, chop 2 medium potatoes into bite-size pieces and fry them along with the cauliflower, following the rest of the recipe as directed. Keep in mind that it may take an extra 10–15 minutes to cook the potatoes completely through.

*Chop the Cauliflower*

- Cut the cauliflower florets into bite-size pieces to shorten the cooking time.

- You can place the florets in a bowl of cold water for 3–5 minutes to keep the cauliflower fresh and crisp.

*Cook the Cauliflower*

- Thoroughly stir-fry the cauliflower with the spices to make sure they are mixed well.

- Once the peas have been added, continue to stir so that the spices can blend with everything.

# STUFFED BABY EGGPLANTS
Baby eggplants stuffed with a delicious spice mix and lightly fried

There are lots of delicious vegetables that can be made to taste even better when stuffed with an array of spices. Vegetables like eggplant, zucchini, and okra work extremely well when cooked this way. In this recipe, a delicate blend of spices is turned into a thick paste and rubbed on the insides of the eggplants. As the eggplants slowly cook, the spice blend penetrates through them, making them succulent on the inside and slightly crisp on the outside. This dish is best enjoyed when featured as the highlight of the meal. Serve it alongside simple and subtle-flavored sides like dal and rice. You want to stay away from pairing it with anything that would overpower the flavor of the stuffed eggplants. *Yield: Serves 3–4*

**Ingredients:**

$^1/_2$ teaspoon red chili powder

1 tablespoon cumin powder

1 tablespoon coriander powder

1 teaspoon garam masala powder

1 teaspoon amchoor powder

$^1/_2$ teaspoon salt

8 baby eggplants, slit halfway through the middle and tops left on

2 tablespoons vegetable oil

*Stuffed Baby Eggplants*

- Make a thick paste of the spices and salt with about 2–3 tablespoons of water.

- Spread the spice paste into the slits of the eggplants and set aside for 20 minutes.

- Heat oil in a wide pan and fry the eggplants for about 8–10 minutes, turning occasionally, until sides are brown and eggplants are cooked through.

## GREEN ● LIGHT

When picking eggplants to use for this recipe, opt for Japanese eggplants that are commonly found at most ethnic grocery stores. A good substitute for the Japanese eggplants would be the slightly bigger Italian eggplants. When slitting the eggplants down the middle, avoid cutting completely through and leave about ½ inch uncut from the top. This will help the eggplants stay whole throughout the cooking process.

Once the eggplants have been filled with the spice mix, let them sit in the fridge for about 20 minutes so the flavors penetrate. This extra time will allow the eggplants to absorb as much flavor from the spices as possible. However, if you're short on time and can't spare the extra few minutes to let the eggplants marinate, you can go ahead and cook them as soon as they are filled. They will still taste great.

### Slit the Eggplants

- Use a sharp knife to slit the eggplants, making sure to avoid cutting all the way through.
- Leave about ½ inch uncut from the tops of the eggplants so that they remain intact throughout the cooking process.

### Make the Stuffing

- Mix all the spices well in a deep bowl and add water little by little while stirring together.
- You need a thick, rich paste of the spice blend to spread on the inside of the eggplants, so be careful not to add too much water and thin it down.

# SAUTÉED BRUSSELS SPROUTS
## Spiced brussels sprouts sautéed with chickpea flour

Brussels sprouts are not commonly found in India and hardly ever cooked in a traditional home kitchen. However, since living in North America, I have tried to incorporate as much of the ingredients available here into my modern Indian cooking as possible. This was one such experiment. I resented eating boiled or roasted brussels sprouts and was anxious to find a new, more enticing way of cooking them. That is when I thought of cooking them with a spice and chickpea flour mix.

The chickpea flour lightly coats the brussels sprouts as they cook and slowly caramelizes in the heat. This gives them a soft, smoky flavor that is highlighted by the spices. You can serve this as a side with some chicken or fish curry and a helping of rice. Throw in a salad, and you'll have a complete, well-balanced meal. *Yield: Serves 3–4*

## Ingredients:

12–15 medium brussels sprouts, cut into quarters

2 tablespoons vegetable oil

1 teaspoon cumin seeds

3 garlic cloves, minced

1 medium onion, sliced

Salt, to taste

1/2 teaspoon chili powder

1/4 teaspoon turmeric powder

1/2 teaspoon coriander powder

2 tablespoon chickpea flour

1 teaspoon sesame seeds

1 tablespoon fresh lemon juice

*Sautéed Brussels Sprouts*

- Soak brussels sprouts in cold water for 30 minutes to open them up a bit. Drain and set aside.

- Heat oil in a nonstick wok and sauté cumin seeds, garlic, and onions until onions are lightly browned. Add salt, spice powders, and brussels sprouts and stir-fry

for 10–12 minutes until they start to tenderize.

- Sprinkle chickpea flour and cook for 3–4 minutes until the rawness of the flour disappears, stirring occasionally to avoid clumping. Sprinkle sesame seeds and lemon juice and stir-fry another minute or two.

### Soak the Brussels Sprouts

- Once the brussels sprouts have been cleaned and quartered, soak them in a bowl of cold water for at least 30 minutes.

- This helps the tight leaves of the brussels sprouts to open and absorb the spices while cooking.

### Add the Chickpea Flour

- As the brussels sprouts cook, slowly sprinkle in the chickpea flour and stir-fry to ensure that it is evenly distributed throughout the dish.

- As they continue to cook, the chickpea flour will lightly coat the brussels sprouts and give them an extra layer of flavor.

# EVERYDAY DAL

## A traditional, everyday Indian recipe

An everyday Indian meal usually consists of rice, roti, a dal, and a vegetable, accompanied by some yogurt, pickle, and a light salad. When you're not in the mood to go the whole mile, dals can be enjoyed simply with rice and a dash of pickle. In many Indian households, a different dal is cooked each day, accompanied with a complementary vegetable.

Chock-full of proteins, lentils are a great addition to a vegetarian diet. Add a handful to your stews and soups for an extra burst of nutrition. Lentils can easily take on varied flavors and add richness to your daily meals. That's what is so special about including dals in your meal plans. Not much of an effort where the cooking is concerned, and yet you can have variety in your meals simply by alternating the kinds of lentils you use.
*Yield: Serves 3–4*

### Ingredients:

1 cup red lentils

2 cups water

1 tablespoon vegetable oil

1 teaspoon cumin seeds

2 garlic cloves, sliced

1 medium onion, finely chopped

1 medium tomato, finely chopped

1/4 teaspoon turmeric powder

1/2 teaspoon red chili powder

Salt, to taste

*Everyday Dal*

- Boil the lentils in the water until they become tender and start to break. Set aside without draining the lentils.

- Heat oil in a deep pan and sauté cumin seeds, garlic, and onions until the onions are lightly browned.

Add tomatoes and spice powders and cook until the tomatoes are soft.

- Add cooked dal, season with salt, and let come to a full boil. Remove from heat and serve immediately.

I like to make a big pot of dal and freeze a batch for busy nights when I'm not in much of a mood to cook. Dal, like most stews, freezes well and can be stored in the freezer for up to a week. When you are ready to reheat and serve the dal, simply let it thaw overnight in the fridge and come to room temperature before warming it in the microwave.

To increase the heat level of this recipe, add chopped fresh green chilies while the dal is cooking. As the dal cooks, the heat from the chilies will release into it and the flavor will intensify. Another way to introduce a robust spiciness to this recipe is to add 2–3 dried red chilies along with the onions. As the chilies start to fry and turn darker in color, they will impart their spiciness throughout the dal.

## *Rinse the Lentils*

- Make sure to rinse the lentils thoroughly to get rid of any dust or added particles when using dried lentils.

- The red split lentils are most commonly used in most

Indian homes and require no pre-soaking whatsoever. This type of lentils is usually found in everyday meals and makes a quick go-to dish when you're running short of time.

## *Add Cooked Dal*

- Be careful not to drain out the lentils once they have softened.

- Make sure you continue to stir the onions while frying to prevent them from burning or turning too dark.

# MIXED VEGETABLE DAL
## A highly nutritious dish of mixed vegetables and lentils

This recipe is inspired by the traditional Indian dish called Dhansak, which is a blend of lentils cooked with an array of mixed vegetables. You can vary the recipe to make use of different seasonal vegetables. Veggies like peppers, zucchini, potatoes, and pumpkin would work extremely well cooked this way.

This dish is best enjoyed when served with plain basmati rice and a raita on the side. If you plan to serve it at a dinner party, accompany it with a rich chicken or lamb curry, a flavorful pilaf, a dry vegetable dish, and some raita or salad on the side. *Yield: Serves 3–4*

## Ingredients:

1 cup red lentils

1 cup cauliflower florets

1 cup chopped carrots

2 cups water

1 tablespoon vegetable oil

1 teaspoon cumin seeds

2 garlic cloves, sliced

1 medium onion, finely chopped

1 medium tomato, finely chopped

1/4 teaspoon turmeric powder

1/2 teaspoon red chili powder

1 cup frozen peas, thawed

Salt, to taste

1 tablespoon fresh lemon juice

*Mixed Vegetable Dal*

- Boil the lentils, cauliflower, and carrots in the water until they become tender. Set aside without draining.

- Heat oil in a deep pan and sauté cumin seeds, garlic, and onions until the onions are lightly browned. Add tomatoes and spice powders and cook until soft.

- Add cooked dal and vegetables, peas, and salt and let come to a full boil. Remove from heat and serve immediately.

## Prepare the Vegetables

- When chopping vegetables for this recipe, cut them into similar-sized pieces to allow them to cook evenly.

- You can vary the vegetables according to their availability throughout the seasons to include such veggies as pumpkin, squash, peppers, and zucchini.

## Boil the Lentils

- Red lentils cook fairly quickly and do not take much time to boil through and soften.

- When cooking lentils, always simmer them over low heat to prevent them from frothing and boiling over. Skim excess froth off the top and discard.

133

# CREAMY BLACK LENTILS

## A quick and lighter version of the classic Dal Makhani

Dal Makhani is a highly popular Indian dish that is also a favorite on restaurant menus around the globe. Although the traditional recipe requires the addition of cream to give the dish its rich and creamy consistency, my version makes use of a splash of low-fat milk. You hardly miss the cream in this recipe, as the milk provides the rich flavor and the creamy texture is acquired from the lentils themselves. Substituting

milk for the rich cream makes this dish much lighter and doable for a regular weeknight dinner.

This dish is best enjoyed when served with grilled tandoori chicken or kebabs, some naan, and a flavorful pilaf for an exotic and special meal. *Yield: Serves 3–4*

### Ingredients:

2 tablespoons vegetable oil

1 large onion, finely chopped

1 teaspoon minced ginger

1 teaspoon minced garlic

1 medium tomato, finely chopped

$1/2$ teaspoon red chili powder

$1/2$ cup whole black lentils, soaked overnight and drained

2 cups water

Salt, to taste

2 tablespoons low-fat milk

*Creamy Black Lentils*

- Heat the oil in a pressure cooker and sauté onions, ginger, and garlic.

- Add tomatoes, chili powder, lentils, water, and salt and cook on full pressure 15–20 minutes until lentils turn soft.

- Stir in milk and let come to a complete boil. Remove from heat and serve immediately.

Black lentils can be easily found at most regular grocery stores and ethnic stores. You will need to soak the lentils in water overnight to absorb moisture and plump up. When selecting lentils to cook, pick through them to get rid of any tiny rocks or additives that they may contain.

This recipe calls for a pressure cooker to drastically cut down on the cooking time. Black lentils take a long time to cook and soften, and using a pressure cooker makes it easy to do so in considerably less time. If you don't have a pressure cooker, however, you can cook this recipe on a stove top in a large pot, but it will take almost twice the amount of time and you will need to continuously check the level of moisture to prevent the lentils from dying out.

## Soak the Lentils

- Soaking black lentils in a bowlful of water overnight or at least for a few hours allows them to absorb moisture and plump up.

- Soaking also cuts down on the cooking time.

## Add the Milk

- Substituting low-fat milk for the thick cream traditionally used in this recipe reduces its fat content and makes this dish much lighter.

# RED KIDNEY BEANS CURRY
## A hearty curry for a simple, quick weeknight meal

This curry, which is commonly known as Rajma Masala in Indian culinary terms, is a go-to staple in many parts of Northern India. Since a large part of the Indian subcontinent primarily consists of vegetarians, beans and lentils play a grand role as one of the main sources of protein in the Indian diet.

While most traditional Indian kitchens would usually cook this dish using dried kidney beans, which is then left to slow cook for over an hour till the beans are tender, taking the help of canned beans can drastically reduce cooking time and make this perfect for a simple weeknight dinner. *Yield: Serves 3–4*

### Ingredients:

2 tablespoons vegetable oil

1 teaspoon cumin seeds

1 large onion, finely chopped

1 teaspoon minced ginger

1 teaspoon minced garlic

1 medium tomato, finely chopped

1/2 teaspoon red chili powder

1 teaspoon coriander powder

1 can red kidney beans, drained and rinsed

2 cups water

Salt, to taste

*Red Kidney Beans Curry*

- Heat oil in a deep pan and sauté cumin seeds, onions, ginger, and garlic until the onions are lightly browned.

- Add tomatoes and spice powders and cook until tomatoes soften and pulp.

- Stir in beans, water, and salt and cook 15–20 minutes until beans turn soft.

Red kidney beans can be easily found at most regular grocery stores sold either in cans or dried form. When using the dried version of kidney beans, you will need to soak them in a large bowl of water overnight to enable them to absorb moisture and plump up. Drain and rinse thoroughly before adding into the pot.

To adapt this recipe to dried kidney beans, you will have to let them cook covered over a low heat. Keep in mind that the pre-soaked dried beans will take over twice the regular cooking time, and will also need an extra cup or two of water to slowly simmer in.

*Red Kidney Beans Rinsed*

- It is important to thoroughly rinse and drain the kidney beans before adding them into the pot.

- This step ensures that any excess sodium or preservatives are washed off and do not remain in the beans.

*Frying Onions*

- While any kind of onion, yellow, white, or purple, can be used for this recipe, the purple onion will add a subtle tinge of sweetness to the curry and stand up well to the flavor of the kidney beans.

- Make sure you continue to stir the onions while frying to prevent them from burning or turning too dark.

# CHICKPEAS WITH POTATOES

## The classic Chana Masala simplified for a quick, no fuss everyday dinner

Chana Masala is most commonly eaten in India during weekends as a hearty brunch. Paired with Puris, a deep-fried puffy bread, they make a wonderful start to a lazy, relaxed Sunday.

Since we are not in the habit of eating something as rich and filling during the early half of the day, I like to whip this up during dinnertime. Paired with a side of plain Basmati rice and a simple salad, this dish will make a regular weeknight meal feel special. It is also one of my favorite dishes to serve at a party or a potluck, as is always a crowd pleaser. *Yield: Serves 3–4*

### Ingredients:

2 tablespoons vegetable oil

1 teaspoon cumin seeds

1 medium onion, finely chopped

1 large potato, cubed

1/2 teaspoon red chili powder

1 teaspoon coriander powder

1 teaspoon garam masala powder

1 medium tomato, finely chopped

1 can chickpeas, drained and rinsed

1 cup water

Salt, to taste

*Chickpeas with Potatoes*

- Heat oil in a deep pan and sauté cumin seeds, onions, and potatoes until the potatoes are lightly browned and partially cooked.

- Add spice powders, tomatoes, chickpeas, water, and salt. Simmer covered until potatoes are cooked through, about 20–25 minutes.

Chickpeas make a wonderful addition to any dinner menu. It has a rich and hearty texture that can stand up to any kind of meat and will make a nice addition to any table for vegetarians. As with most curries, this dish tastes even better the next day since it gives a chance for all the flavors to blend and intensify with time.

This dish also stores really well in the freezer, and an extra batch can be made to freeze for later. Let the dish defrost in the fridge overnight and heat it to a complete boil before serving.

## Fry the Potatoes

- Once you have chopped the potatoes, let them soak in a large bowl of cold water until you are ready to add them into the pan. This will ensure that the potatoes do not turn brown in color as well as get rid of any excess starch.

- Before adding the potatoes into the pan for frying, make sure to drain completely.

## Add in Chickpeas

- It is important to thoroughly rinse and drain the chick peas before adding them into the pot.

- This step ensures that any excess sodium or preservatives are washed off and do not remain in them.

# BLACK-EYED PEAS & COCONUT CURRY
## A delightful blend of flavor and texture

I find that black-eyed peas have a much more robust flavor than that of the red kidney bean. Pairing it with coconut milk in the curry, gives this dish a nice depth of flavor. The sweetness of the coconut milk plays in well with the sturdy bite of the bean and complements it in both texture and taste.

While you can easily find cans of black-eyed peas in most regular grocery stores as well as specialty ethnic ones, substitute them with pinto beans if not available. Pinto beans have a more subtle flavor as compared to black-eyed peas, but will also taste great in this recipe. *Yield: Serves 3–4*

**Ingredients:**

2 tablespoons vegetable oil

1 medium onion, finely chopped

1 teaspoon minced garlic

1 teaspoon minced ginger

$1/4$ teaspoon turmeric powder

$1/2$ teaspoon red chili powder

$1/2$ teaspoon coriander powder

1 large tomato, finely chopped

1 can black-eyed peas, drained and rinsed

1 cup coconut milk

1 cup water

Salt, to taste

*Black-Eyed Peas and Coconut Curry*

- Heat oil in a deep pan and sauté onions, garlic, and ginger until tender and onions are lightly browned.

- Add spices, tomatoes, black-eyed peas, coconut milk, water, and salt. Cook covered until peas turn soft, about 15–20 minutes.

Canned coconut milk is readily available at most grocery stores, usually in the baking or international foods aisle. These days many stores also carry a light version of coconut milk, which has less fat content and works equally well as a substitute for regular coconut milk in any recipe.

If a can of black-eyed peas is hard to find or unavailable at your store, you can substitute it with pinto or white kidney beans instead. These beans are often light in flavor and will blend well with the smooth taste of the coconut milk. Avoid using robust flavored beans like red kidney or lima beans, since they will overpower the mild coconut taste.

### Black-Eyed Peas

- It is important to thoroughly rinse and drain the black-eyed peas before adding them into the pot.

- This step ensures that any excess sodium or preservatives are washed off and do not remain in them.

### Simmer the Curry

- To adapt this recipe to dried black-eyed peas, you will have to let them cook covered over a low heat, after letting them soak in water overnight.

- Keep in mind that the pre-soaked dried beans will take over twice the regular cooking time, and will also need an extra cup or two of water to slowly simmer in.

# EGG CURRY

## A simple and delightful way to use a regular breakfast ingredient as a pick for dinner

Eggs are a simple and quick way to include some much-needed protein in an everyday meal. You can always boil a couple of extra eggs during breakfast and jazz them up in a curry for a later meal.

If nothing else, I usually always have a carton of eggs in the fridge, and often find myself trying to incorporate them into my meals. This curry is a wonderful, quick way to take this breakfast item to a new level and introduce it to new flavors. Serve this curry with a side of plain white rice or fresh roti as well as some salad and maybe a dal. *Yield: Serves 3–4*

**Ingredients:**

1 tablespoon vegetable oil

1 teaspoon mustard seeds

1 large onion, finely chopped

1 tablespoon minced garlic

1/4 teaspoon red chili powder

1/4 teaspoon turmeric powder

1 teaspoon coriander powder

1/2 teaspoon garam masala powder

2 large tomatoes, finely chopped

1 tablespoon tomato paste

Water, 3/4 cup water, or more as needed

Salt, to taste

4 hard-boiled eggs, cut in halves

*Egg Curry*

- Heat oil in a deep pan and sauté mustard seeds, onions, and garlic until soft and fragrant.

- Add spice powders and tomatoes and cook 5–6 minutes until tomatoes pulp. Stir in tomato paste and about ¾ cup water and boil.

- Reduce heat to a simmer, season with salt, and add eggs.

When making this dish for a large crowd, you can boil the eggs in advance and keep them in the fridge until you are ready to cook the curry. The curry will also keep very well in the freezer to save for a later date. Simply store it in an airtight freezer-friendly container and warm it up in the microwave right before serving.

To bump up the nutritional value of this recipe and make it heartier for a larger crowd, add vegetables like potatoes, peas, and carrots. Be sure to chop the potatoes and carrots into small, bite-size pieces to enable even cooking throughout. You will also have to cook the potatoes and carrots in the curry for 15–20 minutes before adding the eggs to allow them to soften.

## *Boil the Eggs*

- Boil the eggs until the yoke is completely cooked; otherwise, it will run into the curry.
- Let the eggs cool to room temperature, then cut them in half with a sharp, wet knife to prevent the yoke from breaking.

## *Fry the Onions*

- When frying onions, remember to stir them frequently to avoid burning.
- Once the onions start to soften and turn transparent you can add the spices.

# MASALA OMELET
## A jazzed-up version of a simple classic

An omelet in India is never as simple as beating a few eggs with salt and pepper. With an abundance of spices and seasonings in almost every kitchen, it is often hard for cooks to refrain from adding a mix of flavors into something as simple as an omelet.

A regular on breakfast menus in most Indian homes is the Masala Omelet, which includes a mix of onions, chilies, and fresh cilantro along with a touch of spices. I like to roll this omelet in a warm flour tortilla and serve it with some tangy chutney as a quick and filling lunch. You can also serve it with a side of buttered toast and a helping of crisp potatoes as a special treat for a leisurely Sunday brunch. *Yield: Serves 1–2*

### Ingredients:

2 eggs, beaten

1 tablespoon finely chopped onion

1 teaspoon finely chopped green chili

1 tablespoon minced fresh cilantro

Pinch of red chili powder

Pinch of cumin powder

Pinch of salt

1 teaspoon vegetable oil

*Masala Omelet*

- Thoroughly mix all the ingredients except the oil in a bowl.

- Heat the oil in a nonstick pan and fry the omelet 2–3 minutes on each side until cooked through.

**Spicy Omelet:** To increase the heat level of this recipe, add 2–3 more finely chopped fresh green chilies to the egg mixture along with the onions. You can also increase the heat level by adding a pinch or two more of red chili powder. Remember to beat the eggs well to incorporate the onions, chilies, and spices and distribute them evenly throughout the omelet.

**Mixed Vegetable Omelet:** You can add a variety of vegetables to this omelet to serve it as a nice, hearty lunch or brunch. Add ½ cup each of thinly sliced green bell pepper, red bell pepper, and fresh spinach to the egg mixture and beat to mix thoroughly. Follow the recipe as directed, frying the omelet until perfectly cooked through.

*Mix the Ingredients Well*

- Remember to mix the eggs well with the spices and onions to allow for equal distribution within the omelet.
- To make this kid-friendly, simply omit the green chilies.

*Fry the Omelet*

- When adding the mixed ingredients to the pan, spread out the onions so they are evenly distributed throughout the omelet.
- Let the omelet completely set on the bottom before flipping it over to the other side.

EGGS

# SPICY SCRAMBLED EGGS

## Onions, tomatoes, and spices jazz up a plate of super, simple scrambled eggs

When I was growing up, eggs were often featured on our Sunday brunch table. These days, however, they are no longer the usual breakfast fare. Eggs were made to take on more distinct flavors and would always be a welcome treat.

Nowadays, I find myself whipping up this recipe more often than not, and most of the time, it is jazzed up to take on a new form. I love stuffing the spicy scrambled eggs into pita pockets with some crisp lettuce and sliced cucumbers for a quick to-go lunch. Another favorite of mine is to spread them over a flour tortilla with cheese sprinkled on top and bake until crisp, or best of all, eaten with warm roti after a long day at work. *Yield: Serves 2–3*

## Ingredients:

1 tablespoon vegetable oil

1 small onion, thinly sliced

1 garlic clove, minced

1 small tomato, finely chopped

1/4 teaspoon red chili powder

1/2 teaspoon garam masala powder

3 eggs, beaten

Salt, to taste

1 tablespoon minced fresh cilantro

*Spicy Scrambled Eggs*

- Heat oil in a nonstick pan and sauté onions and garlic until soft.

- Stir in tomatoes and spices and cook 2–3 minutes until tomatoes soften and start to dry up.

- Add beaten eggs and stir constantly to scramble eggs and mix with spices.

- Season with salt and garnish with fresh cilantro.

**Scrambled Eggs with Potatoes:** Dice 1 medium potato into small cubes and fry in 2 tablespoons of oil until lightly browned. Add 1 small onion finely chopped, 1 teaspoon minced garlic, and ¼ teaspoon each of chili powder and coriander powder. Fry until onions soften and potatoes are cooked through. Scramble in 3 beaten eggs to combine well with the potatoes and spices.

**Egg Salad Wrap:** Follow the recipe as directed and set the cooked scrambled eggs aside. Warm flour tortillas in a pan and spread about 2–3 tablespoons of the scrambled eggs on top of the warmed tortillas. Layer with fresh lettuce, sliced tomatoes, and a tablespoon of shredded cheese. Roll up tightly into wraps and serve with mango chutney on the side.

*Cook the Tomatoes Well*

- Fry the tomatoes until they start to lose moisture.
- This will ensure that the eggs won't get runny after you add them.

*Scramble the Eggs*

- Remember to constantly stir the eggs with the tomatoes and onions so that they mix well.
- Don't let the eggs sit in the hot pan for too long, or else they will start to dry up.
- Once the eggs have set, immediately remove them from the heat.

EGGS

147

# SPINACH PANEER
## Soft Indian cheese lightly spiced and cooked with spinach

Paneer is a soft Indian cheese that can be readily found at any ethnic store. Since paneer retains its firm texture and does not melt at high temperatures, it is easy to cook with and can be used as a vegetarian option to transform many meat recipes. In India, paneer is generally found in the north and is a popular choice for most vegetarians.

The mild flavor of paneer is perfect to pair with something as robust as spinach, and combined with yogurt, makes a wonderfully light and delicious curry. When good-quality spinach is not in season, I substitute frozen spinach. Serve this with a side of roti or rice for a quick, simple supper. *Yield: Serves 3–4*

*Spinach Paneer*

## Ingredients:

2 tablespoons vegetable oil

1 teaspoon cumin seeds

1 medium onion, finely chopped

1 teaspoon minced ginger

1 teaspoon minced garlic

$1/2$ teaspoon red chili powder

$1/2$ teaspoon coriander powder

$1/2$ teaspoon cumin powder

$1/2$ teaspoon garam masala powder

1 large tomato, roughly chopped

4 cups chopped spinach

1 block paneer, cut into bite-size cubes

$1/4$ cup plain yogurt, beaten until smooth

Salt, to taste

- Heat oil in a deep nonstick pan and sauté cumin seeds, onions, ginger, and garlic for a few minutes until onions are lightly browned.

- Stir in spice powders and tomatoes and cook until tomatoes begin to pulp and blend with the spices.

- Add spinach and sauté for a few minutes until it starts to wilt, then add the paneer.

- Stir in yogurt and salt and simmer covered about 10 minutes until paneer is cooked through.

I often make an extra batch of this recipe to save for a later date. Let the dish cool to room temperature before you store it in tight plastic containers and freeze for a later use. The paneer freezes really well, and the flavors get even more concentrated the longer they sit. When you are ready to serve this dish again, let it thaw overnight in the fridge before heating it in the microwave.

**Chicken with Spinach:** You can easily make a non-vegetarian version of this recipe using chicken instead of the paneer. Chop boneless chicken breasts or thighs into bite-size pieces and add them to the curry at the same time the paneer is called for. Let the dish simmer covered for 12–15 minutes over low heat until the chicken is completely cooked through.

## *Chop the Spinach*

- Thoroughly wash the spinach to get rid of any sand particles that might be stuck to it.

- You can also use frozen spinach. Just remember to thaw it ahead of time, and use half as much as the fresh spinach.

## *Cube the Paneer*

- Cut the paneer into bite-size pieces so that they cook fast and won't crumble into the dish.

PANEER

# PANEER WITH PEPPERS & ONIONS

Tender paneer is sautéed with crisp bell peppers and onions in a light, flavorful sauce

This dish is commonly referred to as Kadhai Paneer in most Indian restaurants. Since the paneer cooks fairly quickly, it hardly takes any time to pull this together. I like to keep all the ingredients prepped and ready to go so that all that's needed is a quick stir-fry process.

On days when you're rushing to get dinner on the table, you can use this recipe as a filling for wraps or sandwiches and serve them with a big salad to complete the meal. If you have any leftovers, they would also work great for a quick lunch. Substitute the bell peppers with mushrooms for a slight variation in flavor. *Yield: Serves 3–4*

## Ingredients:

2 tablespoons vegetable oil

1 teaspoon cumin seeds

1 medium onion, sliced

1 teaspoon minced garlic

$1/2$ teaspoon red chili powder

$1/4$ teaspoon turmeric powder

$1/2$ teaspoon coriander powder

$1/2$ teaspoon garam masala powder

1 tablespoon tomato paste

1 block paneer, cut into bite-size cubes

1 green bell pepper, sliced

Salt, to taste

*Paneer with Peppers and Onions*

- Heat oil in a nonstick wok and sauté cumin seeds, onions, and garlic for a few minutes until onions are lightly browned.

- Stir in spice powders and tomato paste and fry until fragrant.

- Add paneer and peppers, season with salt, and stir-fry for a few minutes until paneer is cooked through and well coated with the spices, about 5–6 minutes.

150

### Prepare the Pepper

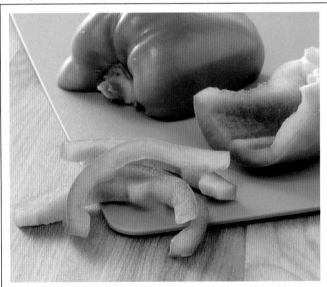

- Deseed the bell pepper by cutting it in half and pulling out the seeds and ribs.

- Slice the peppers lengthwise into long strips about ½ inch thick.

### Stir-Fry the Paneer

- Paneer hardly takes any time to cook.

- Continue to stir-fry it until the pieces start to firm up.

- Use you can leftovers of this dish as filling for wraps or sandwiches the next day.

PANEER

# PANEER & PEAS CURRY

## A deliciously creamy curry with soft Indian cheese and sweet peas

Matar Paneer is a widely popular dish on Indian menus. Chunks of paneer and peas are simmered in a mild, flavorful, tomato-based curry that is enjoyed piping hot with fresh, warm roti.

I like serving this dish at casual dinner parties along with some dal, a pilaf, and a large salad. Like with most curries, any leftovers will taste even better the next day since the flavors will have had a longer time to blend in. Make an extra batch to save for later, too. *Yield: Serves 3–4*

### Ingredients:

1 teaspoon minced ginger

1 large onion, finely chopped

2 tablespoons vegetable oil

1 large tomato, finely chopped

1–2 green chilies, finely chopped

1 tablespoon tomato paste

$1/2$ teaspoon red chili powder

$1/4$ teaspoon turmeric powder

1 teaspoon coriander powder

$1/2$ teaspoon garam masala powder

1 block paneer, cut into bite-size cubes

1 cup water

1 cup frozen green peas, thawed

Salt, to taste

*Paneer and Peas Curry*

- Sauté ginger and onions in hot oil until the onions are tender and lightly browned.

- Add tomatoes, green chilies, tomato paste, and spices. Cook until tomatoes start to pulp and blend with the onions and spices.

- Add paneer, water, and peas. Season with salt and simmer covered 10–15 minutes until paneer is cooked through.

152

Paneer is a traditional Indian cheese that does not melt at high heat. This enables the paneer to stay firm and still maintain its shape while it slowly cooks in the curry.

I often make an extra batch of this recipe to save for a later date. Let the dish cool to room temperature before you store it in tight plastic containers and freeze for later use. The paneer freezes really well, and the flavors get even more concentrated the longer they sit. The day before you would like to serve the dish again, thaw it overnight in the fridge before heating it in the microwave.

## Thaw the Peas

- Thaw the frozen peas in a bowl of water for 15–20 minutes while you get started with the cooking process.

- If using fresh peas, remember to cook them for a longer time until they turn tender, about 12–15 minutes.

## Simmer the Curry

- Lower the heat and let the curry simmer for a few minutes to allow all the flavors to blend.

- Remember to stir continuously to mix everything together well.

PANEER

153

# SPICED CRUMBLED PANEER

## Crumbled paneer is sautéed with onions, garlic, and spices for a quick side dish

This is one of my favorite go-to recipes when I'm in a hurry to make something quick and simple for dinner. On days when I'm not in the mood for eggs and need a good substitute, paneer crumbled up and sautéed with spices often comes to the rescue.

Although this dish makes a great filling for a hearty sand-

wich, you can easily whip up a fancy meal by pairing it with some dal, roti, and a simple raita. To bump up the nutritional value, thrown in a handful of mixed frozen vegetables like carrots and peas with the paneer and cook until they are warmed through. *Yield: Serves 3–4*

**Ingredients:**

1 teaspoon cumin seeds

1 teaspoon coriander seeds

2 tablespoons vegetable oil

1 medium onion, finely chopped

1 teaspoon minced ginger

1 teaspoon minced garlic

$1/2$ teaspoon turmeric powder

$1/2$ teaspoon red chili powder

$1/2$ teaspoon garam masala powder

1 block paneer, roughly crumbled

Salt, to taste

*Spiced Crumbled Paneer*

- Sauté cumin and coriander seeds in hot oil until they start to sizzle.

- Add onions, ginger, and garlic and fry until onions are tender and lightly browned.

- Stir in spice powders, paneer, and salt and stir-fry to mix thoroughly until paneer is cooked through, about 8–10 minutes.

**Crumbled Paneer with Potatoes:** Dice 1 medium potato into small cubes and fry in 2 tablespoons of oil until they lightly brown. Add 1 small onion finely chopped, 1 teaspoon minced garlic, and ¼ teaspoon each of chili powder and coriander powder. Fry until the onions soften and the potatoes are cooked through. Stir in crumbled paneer and combine well with the potatoes and spices.

**Spiced Paneer Wraps:** Follow the recipe as directed and set the cooked crumbled paneer aside. Warm flour tortillas in a pan and spread about 2–3 tablespoons of the crumbled paneer on the warmed tortillas. Layer with fresh lettuce, sliced tomatoes, and a tablespoon of shredded cheese. Roll up tightly into wraps and serve with mango chutney on the side.

## Crumble the Paneer

- Fresh paneer can usually be easily crumbled with your fingers. Make sure the pieces are big enough to avoid their disintegrating into the dish.

- If you find it hard to crumble the paneer with your fingers, grate it using the widest side of a box grater.

## Stir-Fry the Paneer

- Use a wide nonstick frying pan to cook this dish.

- Remember to stir continuously to ensure that the paneer is well blended with the onions and spices.

PANEER

# CREAMY PANEER CURRY

## A mildly spiced, creamy curry that is perfect comfort food

Paneer Makhani is a distant vegetarian cousin of the classic Butter Chicken. I was inspired to re-create this highly popular dish while cutting down its usual cooking time. The version I came up with is perfect for a weeknight meal when you want comfort food without the extra effort it takes to make it.

Leaving out the onions saves on the time it takes to chop and brown them. Pureed tomatoes are sautéed with spices,

and the entire dish is then left to simmer for a short while. This is best enjoyed with fresh baked naan and Chicken Tikka on the side. For a quicker dinner option, serve it with a side of rice. You'll relish it either way. *Yield: Serves 3–4*

### Ingredients:

1 teaspoon cumin seeds

1 teaspoon minced garlic

2 tablespoons vegetable oil

1/2 teaspoon red chili powder

1 teaspoon coriander powder

1/2 teaspoon garam masala powder

2 cups pureed tomatoes

1 block paneer, cut into bite-size pieces

2 tablespoons cream

Pinch of dried fenugreek leaves

Salt, to taste

*Creamy Paneer Curry*

- Sauté cumin seeds and garlic in hot oil until they start to sizzle.

- Add spice powders and pureed tomatoes and cook for a few minutes until mixture starts to boil.

- Stir in paneer, cream, fenugreek, and salt and simmer covered 15–20 minutes until paneer is cooked through.

**Creamy Mushroom Curry:** To make another delightful vegetarian version of this recipe, trade the paneer for 3 cups white button mushrooms cut into quarters. Sauté the mushrooms with the garlic and spices until all their moisture dries up and they begin to brown, before adding the pureed tomatoes. Serve with warm naan or a side of saffron pilaf.

You can make an extra batch of this recipe to save for a later date. Let the dish cool to room temperature before you store it in tight plastic containers and freeze for later use. The paneer freezes really well, and the flavors get even more concentrated the longer they sit. When you are ready to serve it again, let it thaw overnight in the fridge before heating it in the microwave.

*Puree the Tomatoes*

- To puree tomatoes, cut them into quarters and run through a blender or food processor until smooth, somewhat like a rich tomato sauce.

*Add the Cream*

- The cream gives the dish a distinct sweetness in addition to making it rich and creamy.

- For a lighter version, substitute plain beaten yogurt for the cream.

PANEER

157

# CHICKEN TIKKA

## The classic chicken dish baked in a traditional clay oven called a tandoor

A traditional Chicken Tikka dish is made by threading marinated boneless pieces of chicken on metal skewers and cooking them in a hot tandoor until they are completely cooked through and char around the edges.

The flavors added to the Chicken Tikka are fairly easy to imitate, and the chicken cooks extremely well in a regular convection oven or over a grill. This dish is best enjoyed on its own with a side of yogurt dip. However, I often like to chop the chicken into small pieces and wrap it in a warm tortilla with lettuce and tomatoes for a quick, filling lunch. *Yield: Serves 3–4*

### Ingredients:

2 large chicken breasts, cut into 1-inch cubes

1 cup plain yogurt, beaten

1 tablespoon tomato paste

1 tablespoon minced garlic

1/2 teaspoon garam masala powder

2 tablespoons fresh lemon juice

1/2 teaspoon red chili powder

1/2 teaspoon salt

2 tablespoons vegetable oil

*Chicken Tikka*

- Mix all the ingredients in a big bowl and place it in the fridge for at least 2 hours to marinate.

- Place chicken pieces on a greased baking sheet in a preheated 415ºF oven.

- Grill 20–25 minutes, turning once, until juices run clear and chicken is cooked through.

# • • • • RECIPE VARIATIONS • • • •

**Chicken Tikka Wraps:** Follow the recipe as directed, and roughly chop the cooked chicken into smaller pieces. Warm flour tortillas in a nonstick pan and top with chopped grilled chicken. Layer with fresh lettuce, sliced tomatoes, and onions and roll tightly into wraps. Make a dip by whisking ½ cup yogurt, 1 tablespoon fresh lemon juice, ¼ teaspoon cumin powder, and a pinch of salt.

**Chicken Tikka Pizza:** Follow the recipe as directed, and roughly chop the cooked chicken into smaller pieces. Spread store-bought tomato sauce on a ready-made pizza crust, and layer with sliced onions, green bell peppers, and chicken. Top with shredded mozzarella cheese and bake until cheese melts, about 10–15 minutes.

*Marinate the Chicken*

- The longer the chicken marinates, the better it will taste.

- For best results, marinate the chicken cubes in a large bowl covered with plastic wrap overnight in the fridge.

*Grill the Chicken*

- Remember to flip the chicken pieces halfway through the cooking time so that they brown on all sides.

- Use skewers to grill chicken on a barbecue.

- Pierce 3–4 pieces on each skewer and place on a hot grill, turning after 5–6 minutes to cook evenly on all sides.

159

# MINCED MEAT SKEWERS
## These spiced kebabs will soon become a favorite

Kebabs are ground meat mixed with spices, onions, and other flavorings, formed into sausages on a skewer and grilled through. They often vary in the type of meat used, ranging from chicken to lamb as well as fish. It is important to marinate the meat for as long as possible to infuse maximum flavor. The marinated meat can easily be frozen for later use, and I often make an extra batch to save for special occasions.

Kebabs are generally prepared over an open fire on an outdoor grill, but they also cook really well in a high-heat convection oven. Serve these kebabs with a side of naan and raita for a simple dinner, or pair them with a choice of curries, dals, and pilafs for a more exotic meal. *Yield: Serves 3–4*

KNACK INDIAN COOKING

### Ingredients:

1 pound lean ground lamb

1 teaspoon minced ginger

1 teaspoon minced garlic

2 tablespoons minced fresh cilantro

3 tablespoons minced onion

1 teaspoon cumin powder

1 teaspoon coriander powder

1/2 teaspoon garam masala powder

1/2 teaspoon red chili powder

1/2 teaspoon salt

1 egg

*Minced Meat Skewers*

- Mix all the ingredients in a big bowl and place it in the fridge for at least 2 hours to marinate. In the meantime, soak 8 bamboo skewers in water.

- Spread ¼ cup of the meat mixture across a skewer to form a long sausage.

Repeat for the rest of the meat.

- Place skewers on a greased baking sheet and grill in a preheated 415ºF oven 15–20 minutes until meat is cooked through, turning them halfway through.

**Kebab Wraps:** Follow the recipe as directed, and roughly slice cooked kebabs into smaller pieces. Warm corn tortillas in a nonstick pan and top with chopped grilled kebabs. Layer with fresh lettuce, sliced tomatoes, and onions and roll tightly into wraps. Make a dip by whisking ½ cup yogurt, 1 tablespoon fresh lemon juice, ¼ teaspoon cumin powder, and a pinch of salt.

## • • • • • • • • • GREEN ● LIGHT • • • • • • • • •

You can make an extra batch of this recipe to save for a later date. Once you have mixed the ground meat with all the ingredients, put the mixture in a tightly sealed freezer bag and place it in the freezer. The meat freezes really well, and the flavors get even more concentrated the longer they sit. When you are ready to serve, let it thaw overnight in the fridge before grilling it as directed in the recipe.

### Marinate the Meat

- Thoroughly mix all the ingredients together so that the flavors are well blended.

- You can make this a day ahead of time and let the meat marinate overnight in the fridge.

### Grill the Skewered Meat

- Remember to flip the skewers halfway through the cooking process so that they brown on all sides.

TANDOORI SPECIALTIES

# TANDOORI SHRIMP

## Perfectly spiced grilled shrimp make an absolute treat

This recipe for grilled shrimp is wonderful served as an appetizer or a part of a tapas menu. They are a breeze to prepare and take very little time to cook. I love throwing a batch on the grill at summer barbecues. Serve the shrimp with a fresh salad for a light lunch, or add a rice dish to make a more substantial meal.

For best results, be sure to use fresh shrimp, as they are packed with flavor. If you are in a hurry, you can pan-fry the shrimp over high heat until they turn opaque and are cooked through. *Yield: Serves 3–4*

### Ingredients:

12-15 large shrimp, peeled with tails on

$^1/_2$ teaspoon red chili powder

1 teaspoon coriander powder

$^1/_2$ teaspoon garam masala powder

$^1/_4$ teaspoon turmeric powder

2 tablespoons fresh lemon juice

$^1/_2$ teaspoon salt

2 tablespoons vegetable oil

*Tandoori Shrimp*

- Mix all the ingredients in a big bowl and set aside to marinate for 15–20 minutes.

- Place shrimp on a greased baking sheet and grill in a preheated 375°F oven 10–15 minutes until cooked through, turning once halfway.

A bag of frozen shrimp can come in handy when you are pressed for time and need something that will cook fast. For best results, buy large, uncooked, peeled shrimp. They freeze wonderfully and literally take minutes to thaw. Simply place them in a large bowl of cool water and let them rest for a few minutes until the ice melts and the shrimp come to room temperature.

**Tandoori Shrimp and Mango Wraps:** Warm flour tortillas in a nonstick frying pan. Place 2–3 grilled tandoori shrimp on each warm tortilla and top with lettuce and thin mango slices. Sprinkle with fresh lime juice, roll into tight wraps, and serve as a quick lunch.

## Marinate the Shrimp

- Do not let the shrimp sit in the marinade for too long since the lemon juice will start to cook it.
- If using frozen shrimp, thaw them first in a bowl of cold water.

## Grill the Shrimp

- Grill the shrimp until they start to brown along the sides.
- Be sure to turn the shrimp halfway through the cooking process so they brown evenly on both sides.

# PANEER & VEGETABLE SKEWERS

## Soft paneer and crisp vegetables skewered together for a wonderful meal on a stick

Paneer is a soft cheese that keeps its shape and texture and doesn't melt over high heat like mozzarella. It is therefore often used as a perfect alternative for vegetarians in Indian cuisine. Here, the paneer is lightly spiced and skewered with a mix of vegetables. It hardly takes any time to cook through and is perfect on the grill.

You can serve these skewers on their own with some yogurt on the side, or make a complete meal of them by including some naan and maybe a light dal. During the winter when an outdoor grill can't be used, I cook these in a high-heat oven, turning occasionally until they brown on all sides. *Yield: Serves 3–4*

### Ingredients:

1 block paneer, cut into 1-inch cubes

1 large green or red bell pepper, cut into 1-inch squares

8–10 button mushrooms

$1/_2$ teaspoon red chili powder

1 teaspoon coriander powder

1 teaspoon cumin powder

$1/_2$ teaspoon garam masala powder

$1/_2$ teaspoon salt

*Paneer and Vegetable Skewers*

- Place paneer cubes and vegetables alternately on 8 bamboo skewers and sprinkle evenly with spices and salt.

- Brush skewers lightly with oil and place on a heated grill pan, turning on all sides until brown, about 10–12 minutes.

# • • • • RECIPE VARIATIONS • • • •

**Grilled Paneer and Vegetable Wraps:** Follow the recipe as directed, and roughly cut the paneer and vegetables into smaller pieces. Make a dip by whisking ½ cup yogurt, 1 tablespoon fresh lemon juice, ¼ teaspoon cumin powder, and a pinch of salt. Warm flour tortillas in a nonstick pan and top with the chopped paneer and vegetables and yogurt dip. Roll tightly to form wraps.

**Grilled Paneer Pizza:** Follow the recipe as directed, and roughly chop the paneer and vegetables into smaller pieces. Spread store-bought tomato sauce over a ready-made pizza crust and layer with chopped paneer and vegetables. Top with shredded mozzarella cheese and bake until the mozzarella melts and gets bubbly.

*Skewer the Paneer and Vegetables*

- Try to cut the paneer and vegetables to about the same size so that they brown evenly on the grill.
- Do not hesitate to season the skewers liberally with the spices. This will give them maximum flavor.

*Grill the Skewers*

- The paneer and vegetables hardly take any time to cook, so turn them once grill marks form.
- These skewers are perfect as a light lunch served with a side of bread and a yogurt dip like raita.

# TANDOORI CAULIFLOWER

A marinade of yogurt and spices coats cauliflower florets that roast until crisp

In India, where a large part of the population is vegetarian, it is not hard to find simple, commonly available vegetables cooked in creative ways. This recipe is one such example. Although most tikkas and kebabs are predominantly meat-based, there are a lot of vegetarian options for those who demand them.

Since cauliflower is strong enough to stand up to high heat but bland enough to take on any flavor, it is a great vegetable to use in such a recipe. I tried this recipe on a bunch of friends who believed that the only option that vegetarians had at a barbecue party was grilled peppers and mushrooms. Try it at your next soiree, and you're bound to create a few converts.
*Yield: Serves 3–4*

## Ingredients:

1 medium cauliflower, cut into florets

1 cup plain yogurt

1 tablespoon chickpea flour

$1/2$ teaspoon red chili powder

$1/4$ teaspoon turmeric powder

1 teaspoon coriander powder

$1/2$ teaspoon dried fenugreek leaves

$1/2$ teaspoon salt

2 tablespoons fresh lemon juice

2 tablespoons vegetable oil

*Tandoori Cauliflower*

- Mix all the ingredients in a big bowl and set aside to marinate for 30 minutes.

- Place cauliflower florets on a greased baking sheet and grill in a preheated 415°F oven 15–20 minutes until cauliflower is tender and starts to brown.

If you plan on making this recipe to serve to a large crowd at a party, you can save time by marinating the cauliflower florets the day before and keeping them covered in the fridge until you are ready to place them in the oven. This dish should be served warm and fresh from the oven, so it can be left until the very last minute to cook.

If you'd like to prepare this dish more than a day ahead of time, put it in the freezer to keep it fresh until it is ready to cook. Just place the marinated cauliflower florets in tightly sealed freezer bags. Thaw them in the fridge for a couple of hours before you are ready to serve, and once they come to room temperature, grill in the oven as directed.

## Marinate the Cauliflower

- Adding chickpea flour to the marinade helps coat the cauliflower florets well.

- Although the recipe calls for marinating for 30 minutes, the florets could also be marinated overnight in the fridge, or even frozen for later use.

## Grill the Cauliflower

- Discard any excess marinade before placing the florets on the baking sheet to avoid their getting too runny.

- Turn the florets at least once during the baking process to allow them to cook evenly on all sides.

TANDOORI SPECIALTIES

# GRILLED FISH
## Tender spiced fish grilled to perfection

I love a perfectly grilled piece of fish any day, but often find that most recipes lack in flavor other than salt and lemon. Here, I rubbed the fish with a simple flavor combination, and the result was delicious. If you plan to do this over an open grill, make sure you use a firm fish that can stand up to the high heat without falling apart.

You can serve this dish as a main course with a side of salad and a flavorful pilaf. Another good option would be to pair it with some mango chutney and serve with naan. This fish is best enjoyed hot from the oven. *Yield: Serves 2–3*

### Ingredients:

¹/₄ teaspoon turmeric powder

¹/₂ teaspoon red chili powder

¹/₂ teaspoon cumin powder

¹/₂ teaspoon garam masala powder

¹/₂ teaspoon salt

2 large salmon fillets, cut lengthwise into strips

1 tablespoon vegetable oil

2-3 fresh lemon wedges

*Grilled Fish*

- Mix the spices and salt in a bowl to blend well.

- Season the fish strips with the spice mixture and brush lightly with oil. Place fish on a greased baking sheet and grill in a preheated 415°F oven 15–20 minutes until cooked through.

- Squeeze with fresh lemon over top and serve warm with extra lemon wedges on the side.

**Grilled Fish Sandwich:** Make a dip by whisking 1 cup plain yogurt; ¼ teaspoon each of red chili powder, cumin powder, and dried mint; and a pinch of salt in a bowl to blend well. Lightly toast 2 thick slices of bread and place some fresh lettuce, slices of tomatoes, and red bell peppers on one piece. Add grilled fish, sprinkle with yogurt, and sandwich with the other slice of toast.

**Grilled Fish Salad:** In a large bowl, combine ½ cup olive oil, 2 tablespoons fresh lemon juice, ¼ teaspoon cumin powder, and a pinch of salt. Whisk the ingredients to blend well. Add 3 cups fresh baby spinach, 1 cup thinly sliced cucumbers, and ½ cup thinly sliced onions to the bowl. Roughly chop the grilled fish, layer over the vegetables, and fold lightly into the dressing to coat well.

*Prepare the Fish*

- You can use any firm fish for this recipe. The key is to select one that can take the heat and not fall apart while grilling.

- To serve as a snack or an appetizer, cut the fish into bite-size cubes.

*Season the Fish*

- Remember to season the fish well on both sides to impart maximum flavor.

TANDOORI SPECIALTIES

# SAFFRON & ALMOND PILAF
## An aromatic and flavorful rice dish

Pilafs are usually described as rice dishes that are cooked in a flavorful broth with the addition of meat, vegetables or nuts, and whole spices. A simple version, like this recipe, is best served with a rich curry or a heavy lentil dish. The saffron adds a delicate trail of sweetness to the rice and will leave your kitchen smelling heavenly.

When hosting a dinner party, I usually make the pilaf a day ahead of time since it keeps well and the flavors penetrate deeper the longer it sits. Just heat it in the microwave right before serving and fluff the rice with a fork to prevent breaking the grains. *Yield: Serves 3–4*

## Ingredients:

1 tablespoon vegetable oil

1 teaspoon cumin seeds

2 bay leaves

1 cinnamon stick

5–6 whole cloves

2 cups basmati rice, rinsed thoroughly

3³/₄ cups water

¹/₂ teaspoon salt

¹/₂ teaspoon saffron threads, soaked in 1 tablespoon water

¹/₂ cup sliced almonds, dry roasted

*Saffron and Almond Pilaf*

- Heat oil in a deep nonstick pan and sauté cumin seeds and whole spices for a minute or two until fragrant.

- Stir in rice for a few seconds to coat with oil before adding water and salt. Cook covered 15–20 minutes until water evaporates.

- Sprinkle saffron water and almonds over rice, remove from heat, and let sit covered for another 10 minutes.

- Fluff the rice with a fork and mix the almonds in well. Serve warm.

Basmati rice is a flavorful long-grain Indian rice that is readily available at most regular grocery stores. Basmati releases a slightly sweet aroma while it cooks, and when made properly, each grain remains separate and does not stick together. Basmati rice is generally sold in large bags of 5–10 pounds each, but can also be found in smaller, more economical packaging and in the bulk aisle.

To make a perfect batch of plain white basmati rice, use a ratio of 2:1, twice the amount of liquid than that of the rice, and let it come to a slow boil until the rice grains are tender, and the water has evaporated. Once all the water has evaporated, the rice should be cooked to perfection. Fluff the grains with a fork and serve immediately.

## Soak the Saffron

- Saffron has a deep, rich flavor and a little goes a long way.

- Saffron threads are usually sold in tiny packets and can keep for a long time when stored in a cool, dark place.

- Soaking the saffron in water will allow the flavor to widely spread throughout the dish to give it a strong burst of flavor.

## Dry Roast the Almonds

- When dry roasting sliced almonds, be sure to constantly move them around in the hot pan.

- Once the almonds start to get warm, they release their own oil, which, in turn, begins to brown them.

- Nuts can burn quickly in a hot pan, so be sure to keep an eye on them and remove them from the heat as soon as they start to lightly brown.

# CHICKEN & CHICKPEAS PILAF

## A one-pot meal perfect for any busy weeknight

This one-pot meal is perfect when you're pressed for time and need something simple and quick to pull together a healthy dinner. I was inspired to make this dish one evening when I had a strong craving for biryani, the popular Indian rice dish that demands the tedious task of cooking the rice and meat in layers over a low flame. I needed something that would remind me of the classic flavors minus the long cooking time. The rice and chicken cook together in this dish and become infused with the spices. The chickpeas add an extra layer of texture as well as bump up the nutritional value, making this a complete meal when served with a side salad. *Yield: Serves 3–4*

## Ingredients:

2 tablespoons vegetable oil

2 bay leaves

5–6 whole green cardamoms

1 small onion, thinly sliced

2 garlic cloves, minced

1 large chicken breast, cut into bite-size pieces

1/2 teaspoon red chili powder

1 teaspoon cumin powder

1/2 teaspoon coriander powder

1 can chickpeas, drained and rinsed

2 cups basmati rice, rinsed thoroughly

3 1/2 cups water

1/2 teaspoon salt

### Chicken and Chickpeas Pilaf

- Heat oil in a deep nonstick pan and sauté whole spices, onions, and garlic until the onions are lightly browned.

- Add chicken and spice powders and fry for a few minutes until chicken browns slightly. Stir in chickpeas and rice to coat well with spices.

- Add water and salt and cook covered 15–20 minutes until water evaporates and rice is done.

## ····· RECIPE VARIATION ·····

**Chickpeas and Cranberry Pilaf:** To turn this recipe into a vegetarian's delight, follow the recipe as directed, leaving out the chicken and adding ¼ cup dried cranberries along with the chickpeas. When you are ready to serve, plate the rice on a large platter and garnish with lightly toasted sliced almonds and finely chopped fresh cilantro.

## ············ GREEN ● LIGHT ·············

You can keep leftovers of this pilaf in the freezer to save for a later date. To do so, simply store in tightly sealed freezer-friendly containers and pop them in the freezer. When you are ready to serve, let the pilaf thaw on the counter for a couple of hours, then heat it in the microwave to warm completely through.

*Fry the Onions*

- Make sure you constantly stir the sliced onions around in the pan so that they do not burn.

- The sautéing of whole spices with the onions and garlic will give this dish a wonderfully aromatic flavor.

*Stir in Rice*

- Be careful not to fry the rice for too long; otherwise, the grains will start to break.

- The rice will only need to be stirred for a few seconds in the pan to coat each grain with the oil and flavors.

# GROUND MEAT & PEAS PILAF

## Basmati rice and ground meat come together in a perfectly spiced quick casserole

Pairing ground meat and rice in a one-pot meal is a great way to feed a crowd. Top it with some aromatic spice and a handful of delicious sweet peas, and you've got a definite crowd pleaser.

I first tried this dish on a Sunday night when I had a bunch of close friends over. I wanted something that was quick and comforting, and rice always does that for me. I can't remember if I served this with a curry on the side, or just some fresh salad, but I can assure you that it would make a wonderful family meal either way. *Yield: Serves 3–4*

### Ingredients:

2 tablespoons vegetable oil

2 bay leaves

5–6 whole black peppercorns

5–6 whole cloves

3–4 whole green cardamoms

1 medium onion, finely chopped

2 garlic cloves, minced

1/2 pound ground chicken

1 tablespoon tomato paste

1 teaspoon dried mint

1/2 teaspoon salt

3 1/2 cups water

1/2 cup frozen peas, thawed

2 cups basmati rice, rinsed thoroughly

*Ground Meat and Peas Pilaf*

- Heat oil in a deep nonstick pan and sauté whole spices, onions, and garlic until onions are lightly browned.

- Add ground chicken and fry until it begins to brown. Stir in tomato paste, mint, and salt and cook for another couple minutes to mix well.

- Add water, peas, and rice and cook covered 15–20 minutes until water evaporates and rice is done.

## ···· RECIPE VARIATION ····

**Shrimp and Peas Pilaf:** Marinate 12–15 large peeled
shrimp in ¼ teaspoon each of red chili powder and turmeric powder for 8–10 minutes. Stir-fry the shrimp in 2
tablespoons of oil in a deep nonstick pan until they turn
opaque and start to brown along the sides. Set aside.
Follow the recipe as directed, leaving out the chicken.
Once the rice is cooked and still warm, slowly add the
fried shrimp and mix well into the rice.

*Brown the Meat*

- Be sure to break up the meat while browning so that it does not end up in large clumps.

- Use extra-lean ground meat to cut down on fat content. If you choose to use meat with some fat in it, however, reduce the amount of oil while cooking to prevent the dish from becoming too oily.

- Vary the recipe by using ground lamb for a more robust flavor.

*Slow-Cook the Rice*

- Cook the rice covered over medium-low heat so the flavors have a chance to blend.

- If you find that the rice is still a bit underdone after all the water has evaporated, remove from heat, cover the rice, and let it cook for a while longer in its steam.

# EGG & VEGETABLE RICE
## An Indian twist on the Chinese version

Rice is often consumed at least once a day in India, and it is no surprise that there are usually leftovers. This recipe is perfect on days when you need to clean out the fridge or pantry in preparation for your next grocery haul. On most nights when I play it by ear and don't have enough fresh vegetables at my disposal, I simply throw in a cup or two of frozen mixed ones to complete the meal. They still taste delicious, and save on my prep time. You can vary this recipe seasonally, depending on what vegetables are available at the time. The flavor and texture of the dish will change depending on what vegetables are added, but will be worth the effort every time. *Yield: Serves 3–4*

## Ingredients:

2 tablespoons vegetable oil

1 medium onion, finely chopped

2 garlic cloves, minced

$1/2$ teaspoon red chili powder

$1/2$ teaspoon coriander powder

$1/4$ teaspoon turmeric powder

1 cup shredded cabbage

$1/2$ cup diced carrots

$1/4$ cup frozen peas, thawed

1 tablespoon tomato paste

2 eggs, beaten

2 cups cooked basmati rice, cooled

Salt, to taste

*Egg and Vegetable Rice*

- Heat oil in a large nonstick wok and fry onions and garlic until onions are lightly browned.

- Add spices and vegetables and fry for a couple minutes until vegetables are partially cooked.

- Stir in tomato paste and fry for a few seconds before adding beaten egg. Scramble eggs vigorously to mix well with spices and vegetables.

- Add rice, season with salt, and stir-fry until everything is well mixed.

As with most fried rice recipes, this one works extremely well with leftover plain white rice. If you don't have any leftover rice on hand when making this dish, cook a batch of plain white rice a couple of hours beforehand. You want the rice to be slightly cold to prevent it from lumping in the pan, so be sure to give it plenty of extra time to cool and come to room temperature. Firm vegetables like carrots, beans, bell peppers, and celery will work quite well.

## • • • • RECIPE VARIATION • • • •

**Chicken and Mushroom Fried Rice:** Heat 2 tablespoons oil in wok and fry 1 tablespoon minced garlic and 1 small finely chopped onion. Add 1 cup thinly sliced mushrooms and 1 cup shredded cooked chicken breast. Fry until moisture in the mushrooms evaporates and chicken starts to brown. Add spices, tomato paste, and rice and stir-fry.

### Scramble in the Eggs

- Make sure you stir constantly so that the eggs scramble and mix in well with all the vegetables.

- The pan should be warm enough to cook the eggs pretty quickly, so increase the heat if necessary.

### Stir-Fry the Rice

- This recipe is best suited for leftover rice cooked a day or two in advance.

- For best results, cook rice ahead of time and let it cool in the fridge.

- The rice should be completely cooled to avoid clumping while stir-frying.

# TOMATO & CILANTRO RICE

## A mildly spiced rice dish sautéed with fresh tomatoes

I love to make this dish in the peak of summer when tomatoes are at their freshest. In the southern part of India, where rice is a part of almost every meal, including lunch and breakfast, a variety of spices and vegetables are used to create various dishes.

The curry leaves add a fragrant touch to the overall flavor of this simple dish. Often, I also throw in a handful of mixed beans or frozen peas and carrots to turn this into a more balanced meal. *Yield: Serves 3–4*

## Ingredients:

2 tablespoons vegetable oil

1 teaspoon mustard seeds

5–6 fresh curry leaves

1 medium onion, finely chopped

1/2 teaspoon red chili powder

1/2 teaspoon coriander powder

1/4 teaspoon turmeric powder

1 large tomato, roughly chopped

Salt, to taste

2 cups cooked basmati rice, cooled

2 tablespoons minced fresh cilantro

*Tomato and Cilantro Rice*

- Heat oil in a deep nonstick pan and sauté mustard seeds and curry leaves until they start to sizzle.

- Add onions and spice powders and fry until onions are lightly browned.

- Add tomatoes and salt and fry for a few minutes until tomatoes begin to pulp.

- Add rice and cilantro and stir-fry until everything is well mixed.

# • • • • RECIPE VARIATIONS • • • •

**Tomato and Mixed Bean Rice:** Drain and rinse a can of beans thoroughly to get rid of any excess salt and preservatives. Set the beans aside to drain completely. Follow the recipe as directed, adding the beans along with the tomatoes. Cook 5–8 minutes, stirring constantly, and mix well with the beans and spices. Continue the recipe as directed, stirring well to evenly mix all the ingredients.

**Chicken and Tomato Rice:** Chop 1 boneless chicken breast into small, bite-size pieces. Sauté the mustard seeds, onions, and spices as directed in the recipe and add the chopped chicken breast. Fry the chicken, stirring well, until all the moisture evaporates and the chicken starts to brown. Continue the rest of the cooking process as directed.

## *Sauté Mustard Seeds*

- Mustard seeds tend to pop when heated in hot oil.

- Be careful and make sure that the oil is warm, not boiling hot.

- To vary the recipe a bit, substitute cumin or coriander seeds for the mustard seeds.

## *Chop the Tomatoes*

- Do not chop the tomatoes too fine, or they will break down completely while cooking.

- The idea of this dish is to have chunks of tomato visible through the rice, so be sure to roughly chop them into good-size pieces.

179

# LEMON RICE

## A fresh, bright, and fragrant rice dish with a hint of lemon flavor

Lemon rice is a common feature on many south Indian tables around dinnertime. More often than not, it makes use of left-over rice. The rice is lightly sautéed with a dash of chilies and spices, and topped with crunchy peanuts and fresh lemon juice.

I often serve this rice dish alongside an array of kebabs or grilled chicken. The fresh lemon flavor that resonates from the rice brightens up the smokiness of the chicken and pairs perfectly with it. You can also serve this rice the traditional way—by itself, with a dollop of chutney. *Yield: Serves 3–4*

## Ingredients:

2 tablespoons vegetable oil

1 teaspoon cumin seeds

5–6 fresh curry leaves

1 medium onion, finely chopped

$^1/_2$ teaspoon red chili powder

$^1/_4$ teaspoon turmeric powder

Salt, to taste

2 cups cooked basmati rice, cooled

2 tablespoons fresh lemon juice

2 tablespoons minced fresh cilantro

*Lemon Rice*

- Heat oil in a nonstick wok and sauté cumin seeds, curry leaves, and onions until they lightly brown.

- Add chili powder, turmeric powder, and salt and fry for a few seconds.

- Stir in rice, lemon juice, and cilantro and stir-fry until well mixed.

## GREEN ● LIGHT

This recipe works extremely well with leftover plain white rice. If you don't have any leftover rice on hand when making this dish, cook a batch of plain white rice a couple of hours beforehand. You want the rice to be slightly cold to prevent it from lumping in the pan, so make sure to give it plenty of extra time to cool and come to room temperature.

To make a perfect batch of plain white basmati rice, use a ratio of 2:1, twice the amount of liquid than that of the rice, and let it come to a slow boil until the rice grains are tender. Once all the water has evaporated, the rice should be cooked to perfection. Fluff the grains with a fork and serve immediately.

*Fry the Onions*

- Try not to fry the onions too much; otherwise, they will take away from the flavor of the lemon juice.

- The onions should be tender and only slightly brown along the edges.

- This way they will impart their sweetness and combine well with the tart lemon flavor.

*Juice the Lemon*

- If you find it hard to squeeze juice from a lemon, simply pop it in the microwave for about 30 seconds.

- Taste the rice after adding the lemon juice.

- The flavor should be distinct and fresh, so add more juice if you wish.

# MIXED VEGETABLE PILAF

## A tasty and nutritious one-pot meal that's quick and simple to prepare

Often when I'm pressed for time after a long, busy day, I look for a one-pot meal that will not only be a breeze to get from stove to table, but also something that will comfort me after a hard day's work. And a well-rounded pilaf can definitely do that for you. Pilafs are flavorful rice dishes cooked in aromatic broth with a mix of meat, beans, or vegetables.

This recipe is a wonderful way to use up any leftover vegetables you may have in your fridge or freezer. During summer, I love varying the vegetables to include different colors and textures, whereas during colder winter days, robust squashes and root vegetables dominate in flavor. *Yield: Serves 3–4*

## Ingredients:

2 tablespoons vegetable oil

1 teaspoon cumin seeds

1 cinnamon stick

1 medium onion, thinly sliced

1 large carrot, peeled and diced

1 large zucchini, diced

1 cup frozen peas, thawed

3³/₄ cups of water

2 cups basmati rice, washed and drained

Salt, to taste

*Mixed Vegetable Pilaf*

- Heat oil in a nonstick pan and sauté cumin seeds, cinnamon stick, onions, carrots, and zucchini until tender.

- Add peas and stir-fry for 3–4 minutes.

- Add water, rice, and salt and cook covered until rice is tender and all the water has evaporated.

## • • • • • • • • • • GREEN ● LIGHT • • • • • • • • • •

You can keep any leftovers of this pilaf in the freezer to save for a later date. To do so, simply store the rice in tightly sealed freezer-friendly containers and pop them in the freezer. When you are ready to serve, thaw the rice on the counter for a couple of hours and heat it in the microwave to warm completely through.

*Prepare the Vegetables*

*Cook the Vegetables*

- Chop the vegetables into small pieces of similar size. This will ensure that they take about the same time to cook.

- When chopping the zucchini, remove the seeds in the middle so the zucchini doesn't soften too much while cooking.

- You can also add a cup of chopped potatoes or cauliflower.

- Sauté the vegetables until they are only partially cooked, since they will continue to cook further with the rice.

- You can use any kind of vegetable that is in season for this dish. Just be sure to avoid those that break or mush easily while cooking, like eggplant.

# ROTI

## Classic Indian bread cooked over a griddle is a perfect accompaniment to any curry

Roti is a traditional Indian bread made with whole-wheat flour and cooked on a hot iron griddle. Unlike most breads, roti does not include any yeast. Because it lacks extra flavor, roti pairs perfectly with any curry, dal, or vegetable dish, making it a regular feature at every meal.

In a modern kitchen, the everyday nonstick frying works really well to cook roti. The trickiest part is softly pressing down the edges with a thick cloth to enable the air pockets to fill up and cook through. It does takes some practice, but is not at all impossible to achieve. *Yield: Serves 3–4*

### Ingredients:

1³/₄ cups whole-wheat flour

Warm water as needed

*Roti*

- Knead 1½ cups flour and enough water to form a smooth dough. Set aside for 20 minutes.

- Divide dough into 6 equal balls and roll each ball into 6-inch circles, dusting lightly with remaining flour

to avoid them from sticking to the surface.

- Cook in a hot nonstick frying pan, flipping once and pressing the sides gently with a cloth until they balloon up and cook through.

184

## • • • • • • • • • GREEN ● LIGHT • • • • • • • • • • • • •

You can knead a big batch of dough and store it in the freezer for later use. This enables you to shorten dinner-times by already having the dough set and ready for use. Let the frozen dough rest and thaw on the countertop at room temperature for about an hour or two before you are ready to use.

*Knead the Dough*

- Always add water bit by bit while kneading to get smooth, firm dough.

- Be sure to use warm water to form soft dough.

*Cook the Roti*

- It is very important to use a nonstick pan and heat the roti through completely to avoid sticking.

- Use a thick cloth when pressing the sides of the roti to prevent your fingers from burning.

# NAAN

## A leavened bread traditionally baked in a clay tandoor oven

Unlike the simple roti, naan is prepared with yeast and is often featured in a more special meal plan. Naan is often served at weddings and other special occasions where the rich food served calls for a bread with a meatier texture. Although naan is traditionally prepared in a hot clay oven called a tandoor, it is quite possible to make a version of it in a regular kitchen oven.

Naan is best enjoyed fresh and warm, and any leftovers can be easily frozen, wrapped neatly in aluminum foil and stored in freezer bags. To serve frozen naan, warm it in a hot oven without thawing until it softens through. *Yield: Serves 3–4*

**Ingredients:**

1 teaspoon dry instant yeast

1 teaspoon sugar

$2/_3$ cup water

2 cups all-purpose flour

2 tablespoons yogurt

1 teaspoon salt

4 tablespoons melted butter, divided

*Naan*

- Mix yeast and sugar with water in a large bowl to dissolve completely. Add flour, yogurt, salt, and 2 tablespoons melted butter and mix well to form a soft dough.

- Place dough in a large bowl, cover, and let stand in a warm place for about an hour until it doubles in size. Punch down the dough and knead again. Divide into 8 equal balls and set aside.

**Potato-Stuffed Naan:** Boil 2 medium potatoes. Combine ½ teaspoon each of red chili, cumin, and amchoor powders; 1 small finely chopped onion; 1 tablespoon finely chopped fresh cilantro; and a pinch of salt. Place a tablespoon or two of potato filling in the middle of stretched dough, and bring in the ends to form a ball to contain the filling. Stretch the dough out again, and grill as directed.

**Paneer-Stuffed Naan:** Crumble 200 grams of fresh paneer and set aside. In a large nonstick pan, fry the paneer with ½ teaspoon each of red chili powder, cumin powder, and coriander powder; 1 small finely chopped onion; 1 table-spoon finely chopped fresh cilantro; and a pinch of salt. Set aside to cool completely. Then follow dough instructions from variation to the left.

## Knead the Dough

- Knead the dough on a smooth surface until it starts to come together and become elastic.

- Flatten and stretch each ball of dough by hand to about 6 inches in diameter, and place it on the greased grill until it starts to puff up.

- The grill should be buttered to avoid sticking. Brush the top with butter, flip, and cook on the other side.

## Grill the Naan

- If you don't have a grill pan, you can use a nonstick fry-ing pan instead.

- Be sure to grease the pan well with the remaining butter to keep the naan from sticking to it.

# POTATO-STUFFED BREAD
## A spiced potato-stuffed bread traditionally known as Alu Paratha

Stuffed Indian breads are traditionally referred to as parathas. The base is a version of the classic roti, and the stuffing varies in type and flavor, including different kinds of meats, vegetables, and spices. Alu Paratha, a potato-stuffed version, is a classic brunch item in many Indian homes.

Since they take some time to prepare, I like to make an extra batch to freeze for later. You can half-cook the parathas, then wrap them in aluminum foil and put them freezer bags once they have completely cooled. When you're ready to serve, simply thaw them and fry them until they have cooked through. These are best enjoyed warm served with a side of chutney or raita. *Yield: Serves 3–4*

## Ingredients:

2 medium potatoes, boiled and mashed

1 teaspoon minced fresh cilantro

1 teaspoon minced green chilies

$^1/_4$ teaspoon red chili powder

Salt, to taste

2 cups whole-wheat flour

Water, as needed

3 tablespoons melted butter

*Potato-Stuffed Bread*

- Mix potatoes, cilantro, green chilies, chili powder, and salt and set aside.

- Form a smooth dough with flour and water and set aside for 20 minutes.

- Divide dough into 8 equal balls. Roll out each ball into a small circle and place about a tablespoon of potato mixture in the center. Cinch the ends of the circle together and form into a ball.

- Roll the balls into 6-inch circles. Fry in a heated greased pan, brushing the tops with butter to brown, and flipping to cook on both sides.

## • • • • RECIPE VARIATION • • • •

**Paneer-Stuffed Bread:** Crumble 200 grams of fresh paneer and set aside. In a large nonstick pan, fry the paneer with ½ teaspoon each of red chili powder, cumin powder, and coriander powder; 1 small finely chopped onion; 1 tablespoon finely chopped fresh cilantro; and a pinch of salt. Follow the recipe as directed, using the paneer filling instead of the potato.

*Prepare the Stuffing*

- Let the potatoes cool completely before mixing the ingredients for the stuffing.
- Mash the potatoes thoroughly to make it easy to roll out the parathas once they have been filled.

*Form the Parathas*

- Be sure to seal the edges completely after adding the potato mixture so that the filling does not ooze out.
- To make this recipe kid-friendly, simply omit the green chilies.

189

# DEEP-FRIED BREAD

## A crispy deep-fried bread that's soft and fluffy on the inside

Puris are traditionally a brunch item but are also commonly found on celebratory menus. A classic accompaniment to puris is a potato curry or a chickpea dish called Chana Masala.

Puris are best served fresh out of the oil, while they are still warm and crisp. Nowadays, however, when everyone is pressed for time, it can be difficult to serve the puris individually as soon as each is done. I usually place them on a large baking sheet in a warm oven to keep them fresh and crisp until I'm ready to serve everyone at once. *Yield: Serves 3–4*

### Ingredients:

2 cups all-purpose flour

$1/2$ teaspoon salt

2 tablespoons melted butter

Water, as needed

Oil, for deep-frying

*Deep-Fried Bread*

- Mix flour with salt and butter and knead with water to form into a smooth dough. Set aside for 20 minutes.

- Divide dough into 12 equal balls and roll out each ball into thin circular discs.

- Heat enough oil in a wok for deep-frying and slowly add one disc. Fry until it puffs up and turns golden on both sides, flipping once.

- Strain on paper towels and serve warm.

**Potato-Stuffed Fried Bread:** Boil 2 medium potatoes. Combine ½ teaspoon each of red chili, cumin, and amchoor powders; 1 small finely chopped onion; 1 tablespoon finely chopped fresh cilantro; and a pinch of salt. When dough is ready, place a tablespoon or two of potato filling in the middle and bring in the ends to form a ball to contain filling. Roll out dough again, and fry as directed.

**Paneer-Stuffed Fried Bread:** Crumble 200 grams of fresh paneer and set aside. In a large nonstick pan, fry the paneer with ½ teaspoon each of red chili powder, cumin powder, and coriander powder; 1 small finely chopped onion; 1 tablespoon finely chopped fresh cilantro; and a pinch of salt. Follow the dough instructions from variation to the left.

## Roll out the Dough

- Roll out the dough into thin discs so that they easily puff up in the hot oil.

- Adding butter to the dough helps to easily roll it out without the need for extra flour.

## Fry the Discs

- Never deep-fry more than one puri at a time to prevent overcrowding in the wok.

- To test if the oil is hot enough, throw in a pinch of the dough. If it starts to sizzle and float to the top immediately, the oil is ready for frying.

# SEMOLINA PANCAKES
## A fancy, savory twist on the regular breakfast version

Semolina pancakes, also known as chillas, are traditionally served as a light evening snack with chutneys. However, I like to serve this savory version for brunch as a change from the regular sweet flour pancakes. The semolina gives a grainy texture to the pancakes and pairs wonderfully with a tangy chutney.

You can omit the green chilies to make the pancakes more kid-friendly. Serve them with a variety of chutneys or a light curry for a simple, delicious dinner. Any leftovers keep really well, and are great for lunch the next day. *Yield: Serves 3–4*

**Ingredients:**

1 cup semolina

2 cups water

1 small onion, finely chopped

1 green chili, minced

¼ teaspoon red chili powder

½ teaspoon salt

¼ cup vegetable oil

*Semolina Pancakes*

- Mix semolina and water and let sit for 45 minutes. Stir to blend well into a smooth batter.

- Stir onions, green chilies, chili powder, and salt into the batter.

- Gently pour a ladleful of batter into a lightly greased nonstick pan. Once the pancake starts to turn opaque, flip and cook on the other side, adding drops of oil as necessary.

# • • • • RECIPE VARIATIONS • • • •

**Sweet Semolina Pancakes:** You can make a sweet version of this recipe by omitting the onions, salt, and spices and adding 2 tablespoons of sugar and a few drops of pure vanilla extract to the batter. Follow the recipe as directed. Serve with chopped fresh fruits like strawberries, mangoes, or bananas.

**Semolina Pancakes with Egg:** Make pancakes as directed and wrap in foil to keep warm. Beat 2 eggs with 1 finely chopped green chili, 1 tablespoon finely chopped cilantro, ¼ teaspoon cumin powder, and a pinch of salt. Heat 2 tablespoons of oil in a pan, add egg mixture, and scramble until cooked. Top each with a tablespoon of scrambled eggs and a dollop of mango chutney.

*Let the Batter Sit*

- The batter will thicken once it has sat for several minutes.

- Be sure to mix the batter well so that the semolina is well blended with the water.

*Fry the Pancakes*

- The batter will not spread easily when added to the hot pan, so use the back of the ladle to spread it as much as you can without breaking the pancake.

- These pancakes are best enjoyed warm with a side of tangy chutney and are perfect for brunch or a light dinner.

# BEET RAITA
## Beets add a dash of pink to the classic Indian yogurt dip

In India, a raita is often served with a meal of curries to cut down on the heat level of the food. Since raitas are generally served cold, the cool creaminess of the yogurt helps lessen the spice impact on the palate. There are many versions of the classic raita, each starting with a base of smooth, creamy yogurt.

Beets are a wonderful way to make something as simple as a yogurt dip look exotic by adding a strong dash of color. The subtle flavor of the beets also does not overpower the flavors of any dish it may be served with. Try this simple raita as a dip for crackers or as a side with a pilaf. *Yield: Serves 2–3*

### Ingredients:

1 cup plain yogurt, beaten until smooth

2 medium beets, finely grated

2 tablespoons minced fresh mint

Salt, to taste

Pinch of red chili powder

1/4 teaspoon cumin powder

*Beet Raita*

- Mix all the ingredients together in a large bowl.

- Serve cold.

Raita should always be made immediately before serving to enjoy it at its best. Keeping raita in the fridge for a long time can dampen the flavor and extract the moisture from the yogurt. Also, when using fresh herbs like mint, it is always best to add them to the dish at the very last moment.

The beet's deep pink color can stain your hands, so to be on the safe side, use plastic kitchen gloves when handling them. You can add the grated beets to the yogurt right before serving and gently fold them in so they do not colorize the yogurt completely.

*Grate the Beets*

- Use plastic gloves when working with beets to avoid staining your fingers and nails.

- The color of the beets will turn the yogurt deep pink, making for a nice presentation.

- As an alternative, use grated carrots instead of beets.

*Mince the Mint*

- Mint turns brown quickly once chopped, so make this dish as soon as you're ready to serve.

- The coolness of the yogurt and mint makes this a nice accompaniment to any spicy curry dish.

# MANGO & MINT CHUTNEY

## Robust mint and sweet mangoes come together in this chutney to tantalize your palate

Indian cuisine is known for its strong, robust flavors, and there is no better way for this to come through than in a chutney. Chutneys started out as a way to make use of leftover ingredients that could not find their way into the preparation of the main meal. In most cases, chutneys are prepared fresh, to be consumed immediately; however, there are many varieties that keep fairly well for a couple of days when stored in an airtight jar in the fridge. There was a time when I only used this chutney as a dip with finger foods like samosas or chicken nuggets. Then one day, in a sudden bout of curiosity, I decided to top a scoop of vanilla ice cream with it and never looked back. *Yield: Serves 3–4*

**Ingredients:**

1 large ripe mango, peeled and chopped

8–10 fresh mint leaves

1 tablespoon sugar

2 tablespoons fresh lemon juice

Pinch of salt

*Mango and Mint Chutney*

- Blend all the ingredients together in a food processor or blender until smooth.

- Serve cold.

You can keep any leftovers of this chutney in the fridge, stored in an airtight container. It should keep well for 2 or 3 days, but it is best enjoyed eaten fresh, as soon as it is made. The leftovers can be used as a marinade for grilled fish or shrimp. You can also use this chutney as a salad dressing by thinning it down with a bit of water.

Mangoes are one of the most popular fruits in India, and it is no surprise that Indian cuisine makes use of them in very creative ways. This recipe is a great accompaniment to most deep-fried finger foods, as well as making a nice addition to a spicy curry meal. You can use any kind of mangoes that are in season—just make sure they are well ripened to get an intense sweet flavor.

*Chop the Mango*

- To get the most out of a mango, first cut through its wider sides vertically as close to the pit as possible.

- Then, with a paring knife, slice out the remaining flesh along the edges of the pit.

- This chutney should have a balanced sweet and tart flavor.

- If your mango lacks in sweetness, increase the amount of sugar a bit.

*Blend the Ingredients*

- The consistency of this chutney should be like that of a dipping sauce.

- If you find that the chutney has turned out too thick for your liking, simply add a tablespoon or two of water to thin it down.

CHUTNEYS & DIPS

# TOMATO CHUTNEY

## Fresh tomatoes are cooked down to create a flavorful spicy and sweet chutney

I love making a big batch of this chutney during the summer months when tomatoes are at their peak. When cooked slowly, fresh ripe tomatoes release a wonderful sweetness that blends really well with the chutney's spices. Refrain from using canned tomatoes to make this chutney, as the true flavor of fresh tomatoes can never be imitated.

When making a big batch, store it in airtight glass jars in the fridge, where it will stay fresh for about a week. You can also freeze a batch for a couple of months. This chutney makes a great accompaniment to the stuffed Indian breads called parathas, or served alongside a simple dal. *Yield: Serves 3–4*

### Ingredients:

1 teaspoon cooking oil

1 teaspoon mustard seeds

1 teaspoon cumin seeds

2 garlic cloves, minced

3–4 fresh curry leaves

2 large tomatoes, chopped

$1/4$ teaspoon red chili powder

$1/4$ teaspoon turmeric powder

Salt, to taste

*Tomato Chutney*

- Heat oil in a nonstick pan and sauté mustard and cumin seeds until they start to sizzle.

- Add garlic and curry leaves and fry for a few seconds until fragrant.

- Add tomatoes and spice powders and cook over low heat until tomatoes soften and pulp. Season with salt and serve warm.

*Sauté the Curry Leaves*

- Curry leaves give a wonderful punch of flavor to this chutney.
- Be careful not to let them turn too dark to avoid burning, which will leave a bitter aftertaste.

*Cook the Tomatoes*

- The tomatoes need to cook down to a pulp to give this chutney a thick consistency.
- You can add a bit of water if the tomatoes are too firm to pulp on their own.

CHUTNEYS & DIPS

# CILANTRO CHUTNEY

## Fresh cilantro infused in yogurt makes for a finger-licking delight

Fresh cilantro has a wonderfully mild yet aromatic flavor to it, and when paired with plain yogurt, makes a wonderful dip. Traditionally, you will often see this chutney served with a plate of lamb biryani, a spicy rice casserole famous for its exotic blend of flavors.

I love to serve this chutney with samosas straight from the oven. The cool chutney and the warm samosas combine for a wonderful mix of textures. You should make this chutney immediately before you plan to serve it, and also consume it right away. Yogurt-based chutneys don't keep well if stored for any length of time and will lose their fresh flavor. *Yield: Serves 3–4*

**Ingredients:**

2 cups chopped fresh cilantro

8–10 fresh mint leaves

1 green chili, roughly chopped

1 cup plain yogurt, beaten

2 tablespoons fresh lemon juice

$1/4$ teaspoon cumin powder

Salt, to taste

*Cilantro Chutney*

- Mix all the ingredients together in a blender or food processor until smooth.

- Serve cold.

You can use this chutney as a spread on toast or mixed with warm pasta as a pesto. Since cilantro starts to darken and turn brown when kept in contact with moisture, this chutney will start to lose its robust green color if kept out for too long. Though it's best to enjoy this chutney fresh, if you have any leftovers, you can keep it in the fridge for a day or two, stored in an airtight container.

**ZOOM**

Chutneys can be classified in two basic categories. The fresh, those that are blended with fresh ingredients and spices and require no cooking, and the cooked chutneys, those simmered over a low heat till the flavors are blended. While chutney is enjoyed in almost every home throughout the country, it is as diverse in flavor as the number of hands that make it every day.

*Chop the Cilantro*

- Avoid using the stems of the leaves since they will impart a slightly bitter taste.
- When selecting cilantro, look for a bunch that is as fresh as possible and vibrantly green.

*Blend the Ingredients*

- Since yogurt doesn't keep well for long, make this chutney as close to serving time as possible.
- For best results, use plain Greek yogurt. However, a 2 percent or fat-free version will also work quite well.

CHUTNEYS & DIPS

# SPICED TOMATO RAITA

## Fresh tomatoes and verdant cilantro come together to jazz up plain yogurt

This version of raita is a simple Indian homemade way to serve up a quick salad. In most Indian homes, a raita is often made with a variety of vegetables and spices. Tomatoes add a subtle sweetness to the plain yogurt and give it much-needed texture.

Pair this raita with a meal that consists of a rich curry or lentil dish or a hearty pilaf. It also goes great with the stuffed Indian breads called parathas. *Yield: Serves 3–4*

### Ingredients:

1 cup plain yogurt, beaten

1 large tomato, finely chopped

2 tablespoons minced fresh cilantro

$1/4$ teaspoon cumin powder

Pinch of red chili powder

Salt, to taste

*Spiced Tomato Raita*

- Mix all the ingredients together in a large bowl.

- Serve cold.

*Prepare the Tomato*

- For best results, use a vine-ripened tomato for its intense flavor.

- If you like your raita a bit chunkier, deseed the tomato before chopping it and adding it in.

*Prepare the Raita*

- When mixing the tomato pieces into the yogurt, remember that they will continue to break down and release their juices.

- Prepare this raita immediately before serving to avoid it becoming too thin.

CHUTNEYS & DIPS

# TAMARIND CHUTNEY

## This classic sweet and sour chutney is a wonderful accompaniment to any finger food

Tamarind chutney is a classic dip in Indian cuisine, and often varies in taste depending on the region. While the southern part of India tends to make it more sweet than sour, the north prefers their chutneys to be more tart. Personally I prefer mine to be a balance of both sweet and sour, and with a touch of heat.

If you walk the streets of any large Indian city, you will see vendors selling crispy fried samosas or fritters topped with a generous amount of this chutney. It goes fairly well with anything deep-fried, as well as makes a wonderful spread for sandwiches. This chutney stores really well for a couple of weeks in the fridge. *Yield: Serves 3–4*

### Ingredients:

1 cup tamarind pulp

2 tablespoons sugar

1/4 teaspoon red chili powder

1/2 teaspoon cumin powder

*Tamarind Chutney*

- Simmer all the ingredients in a nonstick pan for a couple of minutes until the mixture starts to thicken like syrup.

- Serve warm or cold.

Tamarind is widely used in many Indian recipes as a sour-ing agent. While traditionally recipes often call for tamarind juice, which is made by soaking dried tamarind in hot water and releasing its pulp, you can easily use store-bought tamarind concentrate as a substitute. Tamarind concen-trate can be found in small jars at ethnic stores, and it keeps well stored in the fridge for a couple of weeks.

## Prepare the Tamarind

- Tamarind is often sold in ethnic stores dried, in the form of blocks.

- To prepare tamarind pulp, soak 2 tablespoons of tama-rind in 1½ cups of hot water for about an hour.

- Break it up with a fork to release any seeds, strain, and reserve the clear pulp.

## Simmer the Chutney

- The consistency of this chutney should be more like that of a sauce.

- If it starts to get too thick, add a tablespoon or two of water to thin it down.

- This chutney can be stored in a clean glass jar in the fridge for up to 3 weeks.

CHUTNEYS & DIPS

# COCONUT ALMOND FUDGE

## Condensed milk simplifies and quickens this traditional celebratory sweet

Festivals in India are celebrated with much gaiety and oomph that includes a wide array of colors, lights, and food. During these celebratory times, sweets and desserts play a huge role in bringing friends and family together. Boxes of sweets by the pounds are generously given to loved ones.

While these days almost everyone simply makes a stop at the local bakery to buy these sweets, traditionally they were carefully made in huge batches by the ladies of the household. *Yield: Serves 6–8*

### Ingredients:

3 cups coconut flakes

1 small can sweetened condensed milk

1 cup finely crushed almonds

*Coconut Almond Fudge*

- In a nonstick pan, heat coconut and condensed milk, stirring frequently until all the moisture evaporates. Set aside to cool.

- Once it is cool enough to handle, form the mixture into golf-ball–size balls and roll them in the chopped almonds to coat.

This coconut fudge is one of the most commonly sold sweets in India. Instead of boiling whole milk over low heat while constantly stirring it to get the required consistency, I simply substituted all that hard work with a can of sweetened condensed milk. This drastically cuts down on the cooking time and makes the recipe quick and simple to prepare on short notice. It's fairly rich in flavor, so I'd suggest eating it in moderation—that is, of course, if you can contain yourself.

## *Prepare the Fudge*

- Condensed milk can burn quickly, so avoid this by setting the heat to medium and stirring constantly.

- Once you notice that the mixture is firming up and there is no more moisture left, turn off heat and set aside to cool.

## *Prepare the Almonds*

- To crush almonds, roughly chop them into pieces and crush further using a mortar and pestle.

- You can also use a mixture of almonds and cashews for a more sophisticated flavor.

# MANGO YOGURT WITH PISTACHIOS

## Sweet mangoes pair with yogurt for a delightful end to any meal

Mangoes are widely considered the king of fruits in India. With the numerous varieties of mangoes available in abundance throughout the Indian subcontinent, it is hard to find a region devoid of its own version of a dessert that features this wonderful ingredient.

I love to combine sweet ripe mangoes with creamy yogurt for a quick and healthy treat after a rich meal. Serve this chilled, and you will never crave that ice-cream sundae again. *Yield: Serves 3–4*

## Ingredients:

2 large ripe mangoes, chopped

2 tablespoons sugar

1 teaspoon pure vanilla extract

2 cups plain yogurt

1/2 cup chopped pistachios

*Mango Yogurt with Pistachios*

- Blend mangoes with sugar and vanilla to a smooth pulp.

- Fold mango pulp with yogurt until well mixed.

- Top with pistachios and serve cold.

**Peach-Strawberry Yogurt:** This recipe can be adapted to incorporate any seasonal fruit, including peaches and strawberries. Follow the recipe by substituting peaches for the mangoes, and top with chopped fresh strawberries as a garnish.

**Pomegranate Yogurt with Almonds:** Beat yogurt with sugar till smooth. Mix in ½ cup of fresh pomegranate kernels and top with toasted sliced almonds as a garnish.

*Pulp the Mangoes*

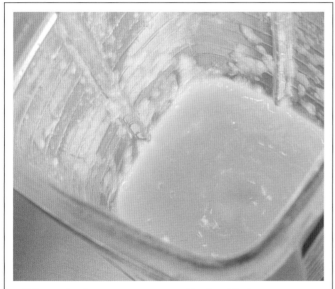

- When selecting mangoes, be sure to pick those that smell fresh and are firm to the touch.

- To give this dessert a chunkier texture, pulp the chopped mangoes in a food processor instead of blending them completely.

*Prepare the Pistachios*

- Use unsalted pistachios for this recipe and avoid the salted shelled ones.

- Roughly chop the pistachios for a more rustic look.

SWEETS

# MASALA CHOCOLATE TRUFFLES

## Fragrant cardamom adds a touch of exotic flavor to creamy, melt-in-your-mouth chocolate truffles

The Mexicans found gold when they decided to pair chocolate with chilies. Then decades later, renowned Indian chefs started to experiment with chocolate, adding a touch of Indian flavors and spices.

This recipe was inspired by a box of truffles I received as a gift from a dear friend one holiday season. Although it contained a mix of exotic-flavored chocolates, what piqued my palate was one particular truffle that carried a hint of spice in it. I could never figure out what the spices were in that perfect bite I had, but I created this recipe to come a close second to it. Serve these truffles after a truly special meal with a nice cup of coffee. *Yield: Serves 6–8*

### Ingredients:

1 cup cream

1¹/₂ cups semisweet chocolate chips

2 tablespoons sugar

1 teaspoon cardamom powder

Pinch of red chili powder

2 cups ground cashews

*Masala Chocolate Truffles*

- In a nonstick pan, heat all the ingredients except the ground cashews, stirring continuously until the chocolate melts. Set aside to completely cool for a couple of hours in the fridge.

- Form cooled chocolate into tiny balls, about a tablespoon in measure, and roll in ground cashews to coat.

**Masala Chocolate Tarts:** If you're pressed for time or can't bother with the hassle of molding the chocolate mix into bite-sized balls, try this instead. Bake ready-made frozen tart shells according to the box instructions and set aside to cool. Pour chocolate mixture into each tart and place in the fridge for a few hours to set. Garnish each tart with a toasted almond.

## YELLOW ● LIGHT

It is best to use semi- or bittersweet chocolate for this recipe instead of regular milk chocolate. The slight bitterness imparted in the chocolate complements the robust flavor of cardamom and gives it a warm, delicate blend. You can get creative with the nuts and use either crushed almonds or peanuts as well, or a blend of all of them.

## *Cool the Chocolate*

- Let the chocolate come to room temperature before setting it in the fridge.

- The chocolate will thicken and firm up a bit once it's cold, and this will help you form the balls.

## *Prepare the Truffles*

- If the chocolate starts to melt in your hands while rolling, pop it back in the fridge for a couple more minutes to cool.

- Continue cooling the chocolate at regular intervals so that it will be easier to form into balls.

SWEETS

# SAFFRON-INFUSED FRUIT SALAD

## Combine the exotic flavor of saffron with a simple bowl of fruit to make it extra special

Fruit salad is a wonderful way to mix a variety of fruits and blend the flavors together. Adding a touch of saffron to this dish highlights the sweetness of the fruits and takes it to a whole new level.

When selecting fruits for a fruit salad, always think color and texture. The majority of fruits generally go well with each other, so don't hesitate to mix them. When in doubt, stick to fruits that grow together in a particular season and you will never go wrong. I like to prepare the fruits ahead of time and set them in the fridge to chill. *Yield: Serves 3–4*

## Ingredients:

1 ¹/₂ cups water

1 cup sugar

1 teaspoon saffron threads

1 cup chopped mangoes

1 cup chopped cantaloupe

1 cup grapes

1 cup chopped apples

*Saffron-Infused Fruit Salad*

- Heat water and sugar together in a pan until sugar dissolves.

- Add saffron and boil for another 2–3 minutes. Set aside and let cool completely.

- Mix fruits in a large bowl and pour sugar syrup on top to coat well.

- Serve chilled.

212

Saffron is one of the most expensive spices on the market. It usually comes in threads of red or deep orange and is derived from the dried stigma of a particular crocus. You will find saffron sold in tiny boxes, and usually not more than a pinch or two is needed to impart its aromatic flavor to a dish.

These days, it is readily available in most regular grocery stores as well as many ethnic stores that specialize in spices. Saffron keeps well for a very long time if stored in a cool, dark place in an airtight container. Always buy saffron that is sold in the form of threads and not a powder. This will ensure that you get the best value for your money.

## Prepare the Syrup

- Let the syrup come to a full boil to completely infuse the flavor of the saffron.

- The syrup will thicken once it cools, so be careful not to reduce it too much.

## Prepare the Fruits

- You can use any seasonal fruits of your choice.

- Adding a variety of fruits with different colors will enhance the look and presentation while serving.

- Top this with a dollop of whipped cream or a scoop of vanilla ice cream, and garnish with chopped nuts for an added treat.

# SEMOLINA PUDDING

## A warm, comforting pudding that's perfect for a cold winter night

Semolina pudding is a perfect way to end a fabulous meal on cold, wintry nights. The warm, creamy texture of the pudding pairs really well with the subtle flavor of cardamom. Traditionally this pudding is served warmed and on special occasions. However, a quick and simple version like this needs no excuse to prepare on any regular day.

You might want to serve a rich dessert like this after a simple meal of curry or dal with rice. The pudding will start to dry up once it's cooled, but a quick reheat in the microwave will bring back its smooth, creamy texture. If you have any leftovers, store them in the fridge once the pudding has completely cooled down, and reheat before serving again. It should keep well for a couple of days if stored properly. *Yield: Serves 3–4*

## Ingredients:

1 cup semolina

1 tablespoon melted butter

¼ cup sugar

½ teaspoon cardamom powder

1 cup water

2 tablespoons chopped pistachios

*Semolina Pudding*

- Cook semolina in melted butter, stirring continuously until it starts to brown and emits a toasty aroma.

- Sprinkle in sugar and cardamom powder and stir in water until sugar dissolves and semolina starts to clump.

- Top with chopped pistachios and serve warm.

**Whole-Wheat Pudding:** A popular variation of this recipe in many Indian homes involves substituting the semolina for finely ground whole-wheat flour. Follow the recipe as directed using whole-wheat flour instead, and garnish with sliced almonds or pistachios.

## Toast the Semolina

- Be careful not to let the semolina burn. Stir continuously, moving it around the pan, to avoid doing so.

- The semolina will turn a pale golden color once it is toasted.

## Dissolve the Sugar

- Wait for the sugar to dissolve completely into the water and semolina and for the water to dry up before turning off the heat.

- This pudding is best enjoyed warm, and any leftovers can be reheated in the microwave.

SWEETS

# MENU IDEAS

Complementary dish pairings for any menu

Whether you are planning a quiet night at home with your family or a cocktail party for friends, try these delicious pairings to create an inspired and lively menu. Also experiment with different pairings of your own. Remember, an Indian meal typically includes rice, a few rotis, a dal, and a vegetable accompanied with some yogurt, pickle, and a light salad. Go ahead and be creative.

## A Quick and Light Lunch

A perfect meal to serve to a surprise guest

- Spiced Tomato Soup

- Tuna Cutlets

- Spicy Corn Salad

## Sunday Brunch

A tasty combination to serve for brunch to family and friends

- Potato-Stuffed Bread

- Tandoori Cauliflower

- Cilantro Chutney

## A Simple Weeknight Dinner

A balanced family meal for any night of the week

- Everyday Dal

- Potatoes with Peas & Cumin

- Saffron & Almond Pilaf

## Cold Winter Comforting Meal

Hearty selections to warm your family after a day of playing in the snow

- Lamb & Potato Stew
- Creamy Black Lentils
- Cauliflower with Peas
- Deep-Fried Bread

## Cocktail Party

Finger food at its best

- Jalapeño Paneer Poppers
- Stuffed Mushroom Cups
- Coconut-Crusted Shrimp
- Masala Chocolate Truffles

## Seafood Lovers Meal

Try visiting your local fish market for ingredients to create this meal

- Hot & Sour Fish Stew
- Chili Shrimp
- Sautéed Cabbage & Carrots
- Lemon Rice

## Paneer Lovers Meal

This menu is great way to introduce paneer to family and friends

- Paneer with Peppers & Onions

- Creamy Paneer Curry

- Sautéed Brussels Sprouts

- Rotis

## Curry Banquet

Entertaining for a large crowd? These banquet selections are sure to be crowd pleasers

- Cilantro Chicken
- Lamb & Lentil Stew
- Eggplant with Yogurt
- Mixed Vegetable Pilaf

- Naans
- Beet Raita
- Semolina Pudding

RESOURCES

# METRIC CONVERSION TABLES

## Approximate U.S. Metric Equivalents

### Liquid Ingredients

| U.S. MEASURES | METRIC | U.S. MEASURES | METRIC |
|---|---|---|---|
| ¼ TSP. | 1.23 ML | 2 TBSP. | 29.57 ML |
| ½ TSP. | 2.36 ML | 3 TBSP. | 44.36 ML |
| ¾ TSP. | 3.70 ML | ¼ CUP | 59.15 ML |
| 1 TSP. | 4.93 ML | ½ CUP | 118.30 ML |
| 1¼ TSP. | 6.16 ML | 1 CUP | 236.59 ML |
| 1½ TSP. | 7.39 ML | 2 CUPS OR 1 PT. | 473.18 ML |
| 1¾ TSP. | 8.63 ML | 3 CUPS | 709.77 ML |
| 2 TSP. | 9.86 ML | 4 CUPS OR 1 QT. | 946.36 ML |
| 1 TBSP. | 14.79 ML | 4 QTS. OR 1 GAL. | 3.79 L |

### Dry Ingredients

| U.S. MEASURES | METRIC | U.S. MEASURES | | METRIC |
|---|---|---|---|---|
| 1/16 OZ. | 2 (1.8) G | 2⅘ OZ. | | 80 G |
| ⅛ OZ. | 3½ (3.5) G | 3 OZ. | | 85 (84.9) G |
| ¼ OZ. | 7 (7.1) G | 3½ OZ. | | 100 G |
| ½ OZ. | 15 (14.2) G | 4 OZ. | | 115 (113.2) G |
| ¾ OZ. | 21 (21.3) G | 4½ OZ. | | 125 G |
| ⅞ OZ. | 25 G | 5¼ OZ. | | 150 G |
| 1 OZ. | 30 (28.3) G | 8⅞ OZ. | | 250 G |
| 1¾ OZ. | 50 G | 16 OZ. | 1 LB. | 454 G |
| 2 OZ. | 60 (56.6) G | 17⅗ OZ. | 1 LIVRE | 500 G |

# FIND INGREDIENTS

## There are many resources available to find Indian groceries

The Internet provides valuable resources for finding quality ingredients, from all different varieties of lentils and rice to hard-to-find flours and spices. Also try exploring natural food stores and specialty spice shops to awaken your culinary senses.

RESOURCES

## Online Stores

### Apna Bazar
www.apnabazarcashandcarry.com
Provides a large range of authentic Indian groceries like basmati rice, dry fruits, premium spices, shan masala, snacks, and teas as well as other household items.

### Ethnic Foods Company
www.ethnicfoodsco.com
An online grocery store that will serve all your spice needs.

### Indian Blend
www.indianblend.com
Online Indian grocery store that delivers to your door, catering mainly to the U.S. Products range from everyday pantry essentials to spices and other goods.

### The Indian Food Store
www.theindianfoodstore.com
Look for chutneys, beverages, and more at this online store carrying a full range of Indian foods such as spices, dals, lentils, rice, flours, and packaged snacks.

### Indian Foods Co.
www.indianfoodsco.com
Online store that offers everything required for Indian cooking, including spices, pantry staples, and cooking equipment.

### iShopIndian
www.ishopindian.com
A one-stop shop for all your Indian groceries, ranging from pantry staples like lentils, rice, and flours to spices and packaged snacks.

## Patel Brothers

www.patelbrothersusa.com

This Web site delivers Indian groceries, snacks, and other household items right to your door.

# Finding an Indian Grocery Store

### Garamchai.com

www.garamchai.com

Browse grocery stores by region in the U.S. Also available is a listing of other online retailers.

### Indianfoodsguide.com

www.indianfoodsguide.com

A resource for Indian recipes, grocery stores, restaurants, videos, blogs, and articles.

### Thokalath.com Indian Resources

www.thokalath.com

Find an Indian grocery store near you. Stores listed on this Web site stock all general ingredients used in Indian cooking like dals, spices, rice, flours, sweets, and more. Some stores offer fresh vegetables.

# EQUIPMENT RESOURCES
## Find equipment through these outlets to stock your kitchen

Start your Indian cooking journey with a few well-chosen pieces. Here are a few places you can shop to find the perfect pots, pans, and utensils to stock your kitchen. From Web sites to catalogs to stores, the offering of products is vast so that you may comparison shop for price and quality.

## Web Sites

### Chefs Catalog
www.chefscatalog.com
Find a variety of pots, pans, utensils, cutting boards, and other equipment at this high-end online emporium.

### Chefs Resource
www.chefsresource.com
Cutlery, flatware, gadgets, tools, knives, and brands like Cuisinart are featured.

### Cooking.com
www.cooking.com
This Web site offers the best selections of items such as top-rated tongs and herb and spice tools. It also offers everything from books to DVDs to a special kids' cooking section.

### Gourmet Sleuth
www.gourmetsleuth.com
A variety of ethnic cookware as well as specialty mortar and pestle sets can be found on this diverse site. Take time to browse the recipes.

### IKEA Kitchen
www.ikea.com
Lots of pots, pans, cutlery, flatware, and small gadgets available at affordable prices. The Web site allows you to shop quickly by category.

### Kitchen Stuff Plus
www.kitchenstuffplus.com
A specialty kitchen store with a variety of products ranging from pots, pans, and appliances to other essential cooking equipment.

## Catalogs

### Chefs Catalog
www.chefscatalog.com
This great Web site also sends out full-color catalogs that feature seasonal specials and markdowns. Order a catalog from the site or call (800) 338-3232.

### Sur la Table
www.surlatable.com
Beautiful table settings and serving pieces are the hallmark of this kitchen store, catalog, and Web site. However, browse the catalog and you'll find wonderful wood spatulas and tongs, as well as other cookware essentials.

## Stores

### Bed, Bath and Beyond
www.bedbathandbeyond.com
Walk into one of the 900-plus locations of this chain and find all the essentials in a wide variety of styles and price ranges.

### Crate & Barrel
www.crateandbarrel.com
Wide range of kitchen utensils, appliances, and gadgets available in a variety of price ranges and designs.

### IKEA
www.ikea.com
If you have a store nearby, shop the market section for great ideas and variety of cookware and table settings.

### Williams Sonoma
www.williams-sonoma.com
Wide range of kitchen utensils and equipment in varied price ranges. Visit the store for seasonal recipe ideas and demonstrations.

# CHEFS & PERSONALITIES
## Instruction, inspiration, and entertainment

Look to these popular individuals and experts for extra tips and training. From books to Web sites, each offers their unique techniques and ideas on Indian cooking. Try out some of their recipes and even consider adding a bit of your own flair by fusing your favorite recipes with Indian elements.

RESOURCES

### Anjum Anand

www.anjumanand.co.uk

UK-based Indian food personality, as well as cookbook author and TV chef, Anjum Anand is known for using fresh, local, and seasonal produce to create simple everyday recipes that are delicious and healthy. Visit her Web site to sign up for an online newsletter and for a monthly offering of recipes.

### Atul Kochhar

www.benaresrestaurant.com/atul-kochhar.asp

Atul Kochhar is known for spicing up British modern dishes with a distinctive Indian twist. He was trained at the Oberoi in Delhi and has been awarded the Michelin Star award. Look for his recipe demonstrations on youtube.com.

### Hari Nayak

www.harinayak.com

Voted top Indian chef on indianfoodsguide.com, Hari Nayak is an internationally renowned chef and food writer. His latest cookbook, *Modern Indian Cooking,* features his signature style of cooking using simple techniques with an infusion of global flavors. His online site offers tips and recipes.

### Julie Sahni

www.juliesahni.com

Award-winning author and TV personality Julie Sahni has earned the reputation as "The Indian Culinary Authority" in the U.S. She offers culinary tours to India. Visit her Web site for details and for information on her cooking school.

## Madhur Jaffrey

One of the most popular food personalities, Madhur Jaffrey is known for her flair with Indian culinary art. She is the author of many cookbooks, including *An Invitation to Indian Cooking*.

## Padma Parvati Lakshmi

Padma Lakshmi is a well-known actress and Indian cookbook author. She is a regular on Food Network, appearing in *Padma's Passport* and as host of *Planet Food,* a documentary series. Also look for her on Bravo as a host on *Top Chef.* She has a passion for all types of foods and is particularly interested in pure south Indian cuisine.

## Sanjeev Kapoor

www.sanjeevkapoor.com

Sanjeev Kapoor is an Indian celebrity chef widely known for his numerous shows and books on Indian cooking. Check out his online site for a great nutritional guide and interesting chef recommendations.

## Suvir Saran

www.suvir.com

Renowned New York–based Indian restaurant chef and cookbook author Suvir Saran is the co-executive chef of Dévi, the 75-seat upscale restaurant in New York City. He has been featured in many well-known publications, such as *Food & Wine* and *Bon Appétit*. His Web site features recipes, spices, and helpful shopping links.

## Tarla Dalal

www.tarladalal.com

Tarla Dalal is a renowned cookbook author and celebrity chef who teaches the art of Indian cooking. Browse her Web site for recipes and special deals. Also look in her books *Dals, Parathas,* and *Curries and Kadhis* for menu ideas.

## Vikas Khanna

www.vkhanna.com

Vikas Khanna is a New York–based chef and cookbook author specializing in Indian cuisine. He offers a wide variety of workshops and classes at his cooking school, the Sanskrit Culinary Arts. Visit his online site for recipes and chef tips.

# WEB SITES, VIDEOS, & BOOKS

## General information on Indian cooking

There are many places you can turn to for help and advice in the kitchen. You can find videos, recipes, and lots of tips and hints online; it's almost like having a cooking school right in your home.

Product manufacturers, books, magazines, and catalogs can also help. You'll be able to find information about products, many recipes, quick cooking tips, and special ingredients and tools.

Online message boards and forums are wonderful resources as well. On popular boards, you will get an answer to your question very quickly. Don't be afraid to ask for help!

## Cooking Web Sites

### AllRecipes.com
Allrecipes.com
AllRecipes, which features reader-submitted recipes that are rated by members, is a reliable source of quick and easy recipes.

### Food Network
www.foodnetwork.com
Like the TV shows, the Web site for the Food Network is packed with information, from recipes to techniques.

### RecipeDelights.com
www.recipedelights.com
From the basics to the specialities, the online site offers tips on cooking and on health and dieting as well as a chef's choice section.

### NDTV Food
http://cooks.ndtv.com
Features tons of recipes categorized by region and ingredient to help you understand Indian cooking in depth.

### Vah Reh Vah
www.vahrehvah.com
A collection of recipes for some of the most loved and popular dishes in the Indian cuisine.

## Instructional Videos

### Manjula's Kitchen
www.manjulaskitchen.com
A wonderful collection of classic home recipes detailed in step-by-step video tutorials.

### VideoJug
www.videojug.com/tag/indian-recipes
Tons of videos that will teach you how to cook some of the classic favorites of Indian cuisine.

### Youtube
www.youtube.com/user/indiancooking
A wide selection of videos with step-by-step instructions on a variety of Indian recipes.

## Books on Indian Cooking

**660 Curries,** by Raghavan Iyer. Workman Publishing, 2008
A delectable collection of over 600 recipes that will cater to any mood, style, and taste buds.

**Anjum's New Indian,** by Anjum Anand. Quadrille Publishing Ltd, 2008
A delightful collection of light modern Indian recipes for the busy cook. It includes suggestions for menus and entertaining.

**Classic Indian Cooking,** by Julie Sahni. William Morrow Cookbooks, 1980
A thorough and delightfully informational book on traditional Indian recipes and cooking.

**Classic Indian Vegetarian and Grain Cooking,** by Julie Sahni. William Morrow Cookbooks, 1985
The second volume to her first book, *Classic Indian Cooking,* offers a comprehensive look at classic blends of curry in the Indian tradition and follows them with accompanying recipes on how to incorporate each curry.

**Curried Favors,** by Maya Kaimal. Abbeville Press, 2000
A wonderful collection of delicious recipes from the southern coastal region of India.

**Indian Home Cooking** by Suvir Saran. Clarkson Potter, 2004
An extensive guide to real Indian food featuring fresh flavors and practical advice.

**Modern Indian Cooking,** by Hari Nayak. Silverback Books, 2007
Recipes that introduce traditional Indian cuisine in simplified forms while preserving the distinctive style of cooking from each region.

**Quick and Easy Indian Cooking,** by Madhur Jaffrey. Chronicle Books, 2003
A wonderful collection of some of the most popular and classic recipes of Indian cuisine.

# INDIAN CULTURE
## Entertaining, the Indian kitchen, and the pursuit of cooking

We Indians are known for our need to treat our guests with the utmost care and generosity, and one common way we all seem to achieve this is through our food. Food holds a very special place in any Indian household. No festivity is complete without a table laden with colorful dishes end to end, enough to please a king.

It's no wonder that out of all the rooms in a home, many Indians take the most pride in showing you their kitchens. Truly, we love food, and our life surrounds it. Our conversations, no matter how they begin, always seem to divert to something food-related within the topic in question. A simple wedding announcement would automatically lead to the designing of the menu. Even meeting up with a long lost friend would be done over lunch or dinner, over food they could reminisce about. I fondly remember my mom working her way through a lavish meal irrespective of how many guests we were expecting. She would always say that it's better to have food left over than let your guests leave feeling unfulfilled. It should be noted that unless you eat till you almost drop, my mom thinks you haven't yet had enough to eat. And so, it is from her that I have inherited this need to cook for my loved ones and feed them till I know they can't be fed anymore.

I started my food blog, Hooked on Heat (www.hookedon heat.com), as an attempt at sharing my creativity and love of food with everyone. What initially began as a food journal with little notes that I hoped would come in handy to anyone trying their hand at Indian cooking slowly turned into a deep passion to impart as much knowledge as I could about the food and culture. Some of the recipes on the blog have been passed on from my mom, many of them have been created by me, and each of them has a story to tell. Like the Shakkarpare made on the morning of Atul's and my first Diwali (an Indian festival) together as a married couple, both of us insisting that we had to start our own festive traditions. Or the Gobi Manchurian I managed to perfect, tasting exactly like the ones found at hawker stalls in India. And especially the Meatball Biryani that I dished up because Atul is not too fond of pieces of chicken with bones in it! Whatever it was, it was cooked and served to perfection, and I hope you enjoy re-creating these recipes for your loved ones as much as I've enjoyed creating them for you.

When I started out to try and impart what I know of Indian cooking, I had a few things in mind that I knew I just had to talk about. I did not want to make this all about the simplicity in the recipes, but instead, I wanted to discuss the essence of Indian food right from the basics. When one thinks of Indian food, the first few things that come to mind definitely include spice, curries, and Butter Chicken. While these may somewhat play key roles when introducing someone to Indian cuisine, it's hard to leave out the other factors that contribute to the rising popularity of Indian food. With that being said, I leave you with two of my most treasured recipes—equally delicious and definite crowd pleasers!

# BONUS RECIPES
Two favorite Indian recipes sure to please

## THE BETTER BUTTER CHICKEN
*(much lower in fat)*

**2 tbsp light cooking oil**

**1 large red onion, pureed**

**1 tbsp ginger-garlic paste**

**2–3 large tomatoes, pureed**

**$^1/_2$ tsp red chili powder**

**$^1/_2$ tsp coriander powder**

**1 tbsp cashew powder**

**$^1/_2$ tsp dried fenugreek leaves**

**1 tbsp tomato paste**

**$^1/_4$ cup plain yogurt, beaten**

**Salt, to taste**

**6 boneless chicken thighs, cut into 1-inch cubes**

Heat oil in deep pan and sauté onion and ginger-garlic paste till it begins to give out oil. Add tomato puree and cook till it starts to dry and thicken.

Add red chili powder, coriander powder, cashew powder, fenugreek leaves, and tomato paste, and fry for a minute or two. Add beaten yogurt, stirring well to blend in, and allow it to come to a boil.

Stir in salt and add chicken pieces. Cover and cook for 15–20 minutes, till chicken tenderizes and cooks through.

# MEATBALL BIRYANI

2 cups Basmati rice

2 tbsp cooking oil

1 tsp cumin seeds

2 cups finely chopped onions

1 tbsp chopped garlic

1 tbsp chopped ginger

1 tsp chopped green chilies

1 cinnamon stick

2–3 bay leaves

7–8 black peppercorns

7–8 cloves

2 cups diced ripe tomatoes

Salt, to taste

1 tsp red chili powder

1 tbsp coriander powder

1 tsp garam masala

1 tsp cumin powder

A pinch of saffron

Fresh coriander leaves for garnish

Sliced boiled eggs for garnish (optional)

## For the meatballs:

$2^{1}/_{4}$ lbs minced meat (I use lean ground chicken, but feel free to use any kind of ground meat)

1 beaten egg

$^{1}/_{2}$ tsp red chili powder

$^{1}/_{2}$ tsp garam masala

$^{1}/_{2}$ tsp chopped ginger

$^{1}/_{2}$ tsp chopped garlic

Salt, to taste

1 tbsp olive oil

2 tbsp bread crumbs

Mix all the ingredients for meatballs in a large bowl. Make mixture into bite-size balls and fry in a little bit of oil till meatballs are brown on all sides. Set aside.

Parboil rice and set aside. (You can use about 2–3 cups of water to cook 2 cups of rice. Just make sure the rice is not fully cooked through, or else the Biryani will turn out mushy.)

Heat oil and add cumin seeds. Add onions, garlic, ginger, and green chilies, and fry on medium-low heat till they start to brown a bit. Add cinnamon, bay leaves, peppercorns, and cloves, and cook for about 2 minutes.

Add tomatoes, salt, chili powder, coriander powder, garam masala and cumin powder. Continue to cook on medium heat till it begins to dry up and starts to give out oil. Add meatballs and cover and cook for 5–6 minutes till it forms a thick, rich, and dry gravy base.

In a nonstick deep pan, put a layer of the meatball gravy, without the meatballs. Now add a layer of rice, topped with a layer of meatballs. Alternate layers of gravy, rice, and meatball till everything is used up. Make sure that the topmost layer is rice.

Crush a pinch of saffron into 2 tablespoons of water and mix with your finger till the water catches color. Pour the saffron water over the top layer of rice.

Cover and cook for 15 minutes on a low flame, without stirring. Garnish with fresh coriander leaves and boiled eggs (optional).

# GLOSSARY
## Learn the language

**Amchoor:** Also known as dried mango powder; added to dishes to give a tart and tangy flavor.

**Arhar Dal:** Also known as toor; a commonly used yellow lentil.

**Basmati:** A long-grained Indian rice that is hugely popular. It is readily available in white or brown and imparts a fragrant aroma with light, fluffy texture when cooked.

**Bay Leaf:** Pungent dried leaves of the laurel plant, usually added in meat-based curries for a heady, woodsy flavor.

**Beat:** To manipulate food with a spoon, mixer, or whisk to combine.

**Blanch:** To briefly cook food, primarily vegetables or fruits, to remove skin or fix color.

**Boil:** To cook food close to heat source, quickly.

**Brown:** Cooking step that caramelizes food and adds color and flavor before cooking through.

**Cardamom:** A fragrant whole spice available in both a small green and large dark brown pod. The small green type is often used in curries or desserts for a delicate subtle flavor, whereas the larger brown type gives out a much more robust flavor and is often used in meat-based curries and pilafs.

**Channa Dal:** Yellow split pea lentils. This is also available in a green color.

**Chill:** To refrigerate a soup or place it in an ice-water bath to rapidly cool.

**Chili Powder:** Commonly known as cayenne; used widely in Indian cooking to impart heat and add a spicy flair.

**Chop:** To cut food into small pieces using a chef's knife or a food processor.

**Cilantro:** This fresh herb is from the leaf of a young coriander plant; crush before using or use as a garnish.

**Cloves:** A bud-like whole spice that imparts a robust aroma and strong spicy flavor to a dish.

**Coat:** To cover food in another ingredient, as to coat chicken breasts with bread crumbs.

**Coriander:** This spice seed is from a plant in the parsley family; the powdered variety is also a very common spice used in Indian cooking and imparts a subtle smoky flavor when added.

**Cumin Seeds:** Also known as jeera; a commonly used spice added to warm oil to impart a warm earthy flavor to any dish.

**Curry Leaves:** Commonly used in south Indian cooking; usually added to hot oil at the beginning of the cooking process to give a slightly aromatic flavor to the dish.

**Dal:** A common word used for lentils, both in the raw and cooked form.

**Dice:** To cut food into small, even portions, usually about ¼ square inches.

**Dry Rub:** Spices and herbs rubbed into meats or vegetables to marinate and add flavor.

**Fenugreek Leaves:** Also known as kasooori methi; is usually added towards the end of the cooking process to give the dish a new dimension of flavor.

**Garam Masala:** A blend of various spices that are dry roasted and then powdered, including bay leaves, cinnamon, cloves, green cardamom, cumin, and coriander seeds.

**Gram Flour (Chickpea Flour):** Also known as besan; commonly used as the base for making fritters or pakodas.

**Grate:** A grater or microplane is used to remove small pieces or shreds of skin or food.

233

**Masala:** The term commonly used to describe a spice or collection of spices.

**Masoor Dal:** Split red lentils. These are widely available, commonly used and quick cooking.

**Marinate:** To let meats or vegetables stand in a mixture of an acid and oil to add flavor and tenderize.

**Melt:** To turn a solid into a liquid by the addition of heat.

**Mint:** A fresh herb used as garnish or blended in chutneys.

**Mustard Seeds:** Seeds of the mustard plant, commonly added to hot oil.

**Nigella Seeds:** Also known as kalonji; it releases a wonderful aroma when fried and imparts a robust touch of flavor to a dish.

**Paneer:** A fresh Indian cheese that can easily be made at home and cooked without melting into the dish.

**Pan-Fry:** To cook quickly in a shallow pan in a small amount of fat over relatively high heat.

**Paratha:** A lightly fried Indian flatbread made with whole-wheat flour and usually stuffed with potatoes and other vegetables.

**Pickles:** Fiery hot condiments made from a mix of fruits and vegetables; often eaten in minute quantities.

**Roti:** A flat Indian bread made from whole-wheat flour and cooked on a griddle or nonstick pan.

**Saffron:** A fragrant sweet spice in the form of threads, which also happens to be the most expensive spice in the world.

**Semolina:** Also known as sooji; a grainy flour derived from durum wheat.

**Shred:** To use a grater, mandolin, or food processor to create small strips of food.

**Simmer:** A state of liquid cooking where the liquid is just below boiling.

**Steam:** To cook food by immersing it in steam. Food is set over boiling liquid.

**Tamarind:** Also known as imli; it is commonly used in a pulp form to add a tart, tangy flavor to dishes.

**Tandoor:** An Indian clay oven used to cook meat, vegetables and breads at high temperatures.

**Toor Dal:** A dull yellow-colored lentil that is most often used as the base for many south Indian specialities like sambhar.

**Toss:** To combine food using two spoons or a spoon and a fork until mixed.

**Turmeric:** Also known as haldi; a bright yellow spice powder used in small quantities to add a rich yellow color to curries and other dishes.

**Whisk:** Both a tool, which is made of loops of steel, and a method, which combines food until smooth.

**Yogurt:** A milk product used in most curries to thicken and give it a rich, creamy texture.

**Zest:** The colored part of the skin of citrus fruit used to add flavor to food.

# INDEX

INDEX

Minced Meat Loaves, 71
Minced Meat Skewers, 160–61
Mint and Cucumber Salad, 56–57
mint leaves, 14, 22
Mixed Bean Salad, 51
Mixed Salad Raita, 203
Mixed Vegetable Dal, 132–33
Mixed Vegetable Omelet, 145
Mixed Vegetable Pilaf, 182–83
Mushroom Curry, 116–17
Mushrooms with Potatoes, 67
muslin cloth, 4
Mustard Fish Curry, 94–95
mustard seeds, 6
Mustard Shrimp Curry, 95

**N**
Naan, 186–87
nigella seeds, 7

**P**
paneer
    Creamy Paneer Curry, 156–57
    Crumbled Paneer with Potatoes, 155
    overview, 24–25

INDEX